Adaptation and Intelligence

Jean Piaget

Adaptation and Intelligence:

Organic Selection and Phenocopy

TRANSLATED BY STEWART EAMES

FOREWORD BY TERRANCE A. BROWN, M.D.

CHICAGO AND LONDON
University of Chicago Press

PARIS
Hermann, PUBLISHERS IN ARTS AND SCIENCE

The original French edition of this work
appeared under the title *Adaptation vitale et
psychologie de l'intelligence : Sélection
organique et phénocopie,* copyright © 1974,
Hermann, 293 rue Lecourbe, 75015 Paris,
ISBN 2-7056-1369-2.

The University of Chicago Press, Chicago 60637
The University of Chicago Press, Ltd., London
Hermann, Publishers in Arts and Science, Paris

Library of Congress Cataloging in Publication Data
Piaget, Jean, 1896 —
   Adaptation and intelligence.

   Translation of Adaptation vitale et
psychologie de l'intelligence.
   Includes bibliographical references and index.
   1. Genetic psychology. 2. Adaptability (Psychology)
3. Cognition. I. Title.
BF702.P49213   153   79-25592
ISBN 0-226-66777-4
Hermann : ISBN 2-7056-5852-1

Contents

Foreword

Bringuier: You've just used the word "biology." Have you come back to biology?
Piaget: Well, I haven't come back to it — I've never left it.

Jean-Claude Bringuier, *Conversations with Jean Piaget*

The problem that has occupied Jean Piaget throughout the whole of his long life took on its particular importance, he tells us in his autobiography,[1] because it was embodied in his parents' personalities. His father was a historian, "a man of critical and scrupulous mind who did not like hasty generalizations and who was not afraid to enter into a polemic when he saw historical truth deformed by respect for tradition." He encouraged young Jean in his early scientific interests and, apparently, instilled in him a deep sense of honesty about what he knew. His mother, on the other hand, although "very intelligent, energetic, and in reality basically good," was "rather neurotic and made our family life quite difficult." As a consequence Piaget neglected play and entered early into serious work "in order to find refuge in a world at once personal and real." Around the age of eleven he became the protégé of an elderly natural history museum curator and began his studies on alpine mollusks. This work progressed rapidly, so that after the curator's death, Piaget was able, at fourteen or fifteen, to publish original articles on malacological subjects.

Up to this point, the young boy's solution to the family situation worked well enough. Absorbed in his studies, he was little aware of the contradictions between his father's stable objective world and the turbulent subjective one in which his mother lived. But this could not last. When Piaget was fifteen, his mother insisted that he undergo religious instruction. This was the beginning of a long and difficult adolescence which Piaget experienced in a way peculiar, perhaps, to genius and from which he emerged determined to devote his life to the work of which this present book, *Adaptation and Intelligence,* forms so integral a part.

In concert with those intellectual changes during adolescence much later illuminated by Piaget, the religious training instigated by his mother had a paradoxical effect. By presenting the "five proofs of God's existence," it encouraged the boy to question something which up to that moment he had never doubted. He saw right off the insubstantial nature of the evidence his instructors marshalled. Crisis resulted, but

---

1. Jean Piaget, "Autobiographie," in *Cahiers Vilfredo Pareto* 4, no. 10 (1966).

was quickly resolved by a book in his father's library. Auguste Sabatier's *La philosophie de la religion fondée sur la psychologie et l'histoire* suggested that religious dogmas are only symbols of that deeper reality which is faith; as symbols they are arbitrary and hence need not be, even cannot be, demonstrated. Thus whatever problems Piaget found with one dogma or another did not need to call into question the faith which dogma imperfectly represented. For a time equilibrium was restored.

All adolescents face, Piaget believes, the complex task of reconciling faith with reason. Faith is necessary to give life purpose, reason to provide some certainty and avoid the pain of contradiction. Never is the reconciliation easy. In his own case it was made more difficult because his parents embodied the two elements in relatively pure form. His mother, irrational and all-believing, distorted reality to fit her needs. His father, devoted to universal rather than to purely personal truths, did not make clear the basis on which life must proceed. Neither solution, at least as he understood them then, satisfed young Piaget.

It was in this vulnerable state that Piaget's godfather, worried by his scientific preoccupation, introduced him to the work of Henri Bergson. Its effect was immediate and far-reaching. In Bergson's equation of God with life itself young Piaget saw the possibility of knowing the first by having knowledge of the second. Biology would explain all things, and would reconcile science and religion. In a freely taken decision to live, he would affirm his belief in God. "By creating a morality based on science... by showing the Good to be a biological equilibrium," he would make that God a universal one.[2] This was the first form of the immanentism by which Piaget achieved internal unity and which in "increasingly rational forms" has satisfied him all his life.[3]

At that point Piaget believed the needed preparation was to take doctorates in both philosophy and biology. He saw then no basic incompatibility between the two and set about his studies. During the ensuing five years he continued his malacological labors, took baccalaureate, *licence,* and doctoral degrees, the latter in biology (1918), and completed everything except the dissertation needed for philosophy. He also began to write: "I wrote even if only for myself" he says, "I could not think unless I did so." What he wrote was an elaborate philosophic system.

Somewhere along the way, however, Piaget began to realize that a system was worth little to him without precise experimental control. The conflict which he had first experienced as an incompatibility between his parents and had next envisaged

---

2. Jean Piaget, *Recherche,* (Lausanne : Edition La Concorde, 1918).
3. Jean Piaget, *Insights and Illusions of Philosophy,* trans. Wolfe Mays, New York: World, 1971.

as a conflict between science and religion now took on its final and lasting form as an opposition between the philosophic and scientific methods. Philosophy, whose basic method is speculation, he had come to see as achieving nothing more than a coordination of values, a coordination which is personal, not the same for everyone, and is irrefutable by scientific means. It does not produce knowledge in the sense of what is true for everyone. Science, on the other hand, provides a measure of certainty, but only in that restricted area where methods of verification have been found. Even if the boundary between the two domains is not once and for all settled, if science extends itself ever more deeply into human experience, still philosophy remains. The need for faith as well as reason is still there: one cannot do without wisdom in the form of a personal solution even while seeking universal answers in the form of science. Piaget's immanentism now took on its final form. He would live and thus affirm his purely personal values, but he would not proclaim them absolute. He would devote his life to science, and there approach the universal. But he would not confuse philosophy and science; he would distinguish his personal beliefs from what he knew.

Where to begin? Life appeared as a succession of evolving forms, each marvelously suited to its environment. Material adaptation in the form of organ systems was not all there was, however. There were also patterns of organ use, behavioral schemes which evolved both in the individual and the race. To understand knowledge was to understand these behavioral forms and the ways in which they came to be. Perhaps the place to start was with organic evolution.

It was as candidate for his doctoral degree that Piaget produced his first work on this subject. In a daring and original study on the common snail, *Limnaea stagnalis,* he came to the herctical conclusion that living adaptation was not to be explained by fusing Mendelian inheritance with Darwinian selection, a coupling which had recently appeared under the rubric "neo-Darwinism." He had clear evidence that the adaptations developed by these mundane creatures in interaction with their environment could, in some completely unknown way and over considerable periods of time, become genetic givens subsequently requiring minimal environmental influence for their development. In this he was not, as has often been assumed, embracing the Lamarckian thesis of hereditary fixation of acquired characteristics through direct action of the environment on the genome. He did not know how it happened, only that it did.

Then for a long period Piaget laid aside his biological studies in order to concentrate on the problem of knowledge. Biological thought continued to play a central role in his work both as a focus of investigation and as a general model for the evolution of adapted forms. He continued to see the transition from organic structures to psychological ones in the innate behavioral programs (reflexes or ethologic instincts) where a genomically determined neurologic structure is coupled to observable patterns of behavior. From these initially given organizations evolve the habits, the various circular reactions, and finally the complex behaviors of the sensorimotor intelligence. But knowledge is more than intelligent muscular acts monitored and corrected by sensation. Knowledge in its highest reaches involves thinking, which for Piaget is action internally carried out. For thinking to occur, things akin to motricity and perception are necessary. But this new motricity should only transform states of mind, and the new perception only "see" and "hear" what is not there. The emergence of the semiotic function would allow this novel form of action, one freed from time and place, from eyes and muscles, and from the world outside. Piaget saw in the appearance of this function the initiation of a novel evolutive series. This began with simple representations of the sensorimotor world, thus permitting the first irreversible forms of thought. It resulted next in concrete operational actions on these represented states, and ended finally with the emergence of the complex formal organizations of scientific thought.

In all of this Piaget invoked evolution, but the strenuous demands of determining experimentally the exact nature of the emerging behavioral structures and the order of their succession absorbed the bulk of his energies for many years. It was no easy task to discover the roots of logic or the beginning of objects situated in a causal space-time continuum in the sensorimotor reactions of the nursling. But they are there, and Piaget teased them out. Nor was it child's play to understand the peculiar nature of the first forms of thought, centered as they are on the subject's person and totally at odds with what is real. To discover the formal structure of the initial operational systems which allow this symbolic form of thought to transform into forms of reason was no less difficult and time-consuming. Piaget's brilliant intuition of the *groupement* structure of these operations alone required twenty-five years to be completely formalized.[4] The conservation of physical quantities, how the concept of number is formed, whence the notion of chance evolves, the progression of the various forms of causal explanation, and adolescent acquisition of the interpropositional operations all required years of dogged experimental toil. Little wonder then that for many years Piaget continued to insist that knowledge was adaptation, that the theories of knowledge corresponded to the various biological theories of evolution, and that the correct one of those theories was almost certainly not the neo-Darwinian one, without, for all that, saying just what was. Evolution in many ways remained throughout this period a heuristic device, useful, perhaps, but only that.

Just, however, as nature has been prodigal in her gifts of genius in the case of Piaget, she also has been prodigal in her gift of time. Because of that, he was able,

---

4. H. Wermus, *Archives de Psychologie* 43, no. 163 (1973).

in 1967, to begin to fill this lacuna in his thought. In that year he published *Biologie et connaissance: Essai sur les relations entre les régulations organiques et les processus cognitifs*. Its aim was "to discuss the problems of intelligence and of knowledge in general... in light of contemporary biology"; its conclusion was that knowledge is an extension of organic adaptation and that its various structures constitute differentiated organs for regulating exchanges with the external world. In this work Piaget also insisted on "the incredibility there would be in lending the most extensive and best organized synthethic powers to the genome, without the multiple regulations in play in turn informing the genome on the success or failure of its endogenous constructions." True, all this is where Piaget had started. Here, however, the thesis was developed and defended much more fully than before and was supported by substantial biologic evidence which had come to light in the intervening years.

The book caused quite a stir. Piaget was accused by several colleagues of atavistic regression to Lamarckian thought and scolded for suggesting that the genome might be guided in its evolutionary efforts by feed-back indicating how things were going. Critics interpreted what Piaget had written to mean that the genome was informed of exactly what had gone wrong in the organism's functioning and even what to do about it. He had in no way said this, but misunderstanding was facilitated by the fact that he had not specified the mechanisms by which he thought phenotypic adaptations might give rise to hereditary reconstruction. He had simply shown that this must be the case.

To clarify these issues the present book was written. Here Piaget not only attempts to provide a specific program by which acquired adaptations can in some cases be hereditarily "fixed," but provides as well biological experiments of his own supporting his conception. Thus, one might say, he has come full circle. In reality, as he admits, he had never left biology. The generative idea on which all of his epistemologic studies have been based is taken up again by the now old biologist. Returning to his familiar snails and reporting new and lengthy studies on alpine sedum, he arrives at the startling conclusion that many of the difficulties of the neo-Darwinian account might be cleared up by reversing the usual view of what is called the phenocopy. If instead of assuming, when one finds convergence of phenotypic and genotypic forms, that the first has copied the second, a conclusion rational only if the role of chance in evolution is held sacred, one were to suppose the opposite, i.e., that the genotype has "copied" the adapted phenotypic form, then a reasonable account of the evolution of adapted forms, both of organisms and of knowledge, might be achieved. To be sure it is not as simple as all that. Many phenotypic adaptations are never "fixed." In all the millennia the Chinese have spoken Chinese there has been no indication that the language is inherited. Apparently the ability to learn a tongue is all heredity need provide. But in other cases, and Piaget provides two, there is evidence that nature does find it worthwhile to reproduce genetically what before has been controlled environmentally. How this is done Piaget here ventures to explain. He then goes on to link this theory of the ''phenocopy'' to the processes of knowledge and all that his researches have elucidated there. It is a vast synthesis and a great intellectual adventure. Whether it will prove true in detail remains to be seen, but no reader will regret having journeyed into this unchartered terrain with a guide so familiar with its challenges and possessing so powerful an intellect to light the way.

T.A. BROWN

Preface

The problem of adaptation to the environment is central to the study of evolution. It is particularly relevant to those issues which arise as soon as a connection is sought between organic development and the development of conduct, including the various forms of knowledge. The doctrine on this subject, which was quasi-official among biologists some years ago, consisted in explaining everything by reference to purely random mutation and selection "after the event." Such an explanation now inspires less and less confidence. One reason for this is that the idea of selection has been subjected to serious reconsideration. It was formerly compared with a sifting process, a simple automatic sorting which led only to a broad dichotomy between elimination and survival. Selection has since emerged, however, as a considerably more refined and complex concept, as regards both its results and the mechanism to which they are attributed. Its effect is thought to be the probabilistic modification of the various coefficients and proportions at work in a prevailing state of genetic homeostasis — but it has a further and subsequent effect upon an organism's capacity for modification, the number of its possible responses, and so on. Above all, the operation of selection is increasingly understood to be bound up with factors of choice, in that an organism chooses its environment as well as being dependent upon it. It is bound also to the teleonomic and regulating systems of the organism's internal environment — processes of organic selection as important as those which remain the responsibility of the external environment.

As the concept of selection undergoes this refinement of definition, the role of chance in the production of variants must, to the same extent, be limited. Selection can then readily be imagined, for reasons of symmetry, as tending to operate by means of exploratory "trials" (known also as "scanning"). Such "scanning" will in part be subject to chance, but can occur only within zones of possible disequilibrium. In considering the thorough integration of elements of the germ-cell, L. L. Whyte was even led to hypothesize that the multiple conditions which mutations must fulfil if they are to be compatible with the overall system will have the effect of regulating them. Similarly, R. J. Britten and E. H. Davidson have put forward a model of genetic regulation to explain the properties of a new system starting with the elements of the preceding system.

It should also be remembered that contemporary genetics has concerned itself only with minor (sometimes very minor) changes in organisms' hereditary programming: changes which are therefore easily attributed to chance. The discipline remains, conversely, quite incapable of coping with evolutionary change on a far greater scale, such as that involved in the advent of the vertebrates. It is of course well known, in physics, that a difference in scale can necessitate profound alteration of the structure of explanatory models. In genetics, present theories are, for instance, peculiarly silent about the basic fact that the genetic programming of higher vertebrates is almost a thousand times richer, in terms of units, than that of bacteria. As F. Jacob, speaking in an interview, put it: "This expansion of the genetic programme... represents one of the great difficulties in explaining the mechanism of evolution."[1] It is quite clear, in fact, that it is not a matter of random minor changes, but of what is in the fullest sense a construction. And this structuring raises the possibility that optimization may occur in the processes of equilibration which ensure living creatures their progressive autonomy and capacity for domination of the environment.

The present study arises from a continuing concern with the question of equilibration in the field of cognitive adaptation, and continues, moreover, research pursued over a number of years into the genotypic and phenotypic variants of a plant species (genus *Sedum*). The question was whether processes giving rise to a "phenocopy," reexamined in the light of these new viewpoints, would not help to simplify certain problems. In broad terms, the phenocopy is a product of convergence between a phenotypic variation and a genotypic mutation which comes to take its place. Its formation is usually ascribed to the genetic processes. P.P. Grassé, however, in a stimulating article which will be quoted again, concludes that "certain phenomena attributed to genetic factors, the phenocopy among others, are perhaps completely different in their origin."[2] A quite central question is raised here which merits close examination, for it raises in turn the problem of relations between environment and hereditary variation. The facts involved are both well-defined in their contexts and far-reaching in their implications.

In broad outline, the solution to be proposed in this study is as follows: (1) There

---

1. [Cet accroissement de programme... représente l'une des grandes difficultés pour expliquer le mécanisme de l'évolution.]

2. [mais certains phénomènes attribués à des facteurs génétiques, les phénocopies, etc., ont peut-être une tout autre origine.]

is first the formation of a nonhereditary somatic variation under the influence of external environmental agencies. If it does not produce disequilibrium, this phenotypic modification is simply reconstituted under the influence of the same factors in each succeeding generation. No further effect ensues and there will be no transmission and no phenocopy. (2) Where equilibrium between this exogenous formation and the hereditary epigenetic program is disturbed, the imbalance will have progressive repercussions. There will be no "message" to indicate what is happening or, above all, what measures should be taken, but the disequilibrium will be transmitted by means of local alterations or obstructions in the internal environment. (3) The hierarchic processes of synthesis involved in epigenetic development may not be capable of reestablishing equilibrium at an intermediate level. The repercussions of the original disequilibrium will then extend to the sensitization of those genes which control the syntheses in question. (4) Mutations or genetic variations will then occur in response. These will partly be chance formations, but will then be channelled into areas of disequilibrium. (5) These endogenous variations will effectively be molded within the framework of internal and external environmental influences responsible for the initial somatic form. Now, however, these influences will act selectively until the new variations achieve stability. (6) These new variations will thus eventually converge, by a process of endogenous reconstruction, with the initial semiexogenous phenotypic modifications. Part II of this study will be devoted to corresponding problems in the development of knowledge. It will be seen there that the substitution of endogenous processes for empirical accommodations seems general at every level of development.

The task of assessing this interpretation must be left to the reader, but first I would like to make a remark about how it is related to ideas put forward in an earlier study, *Biology and Knowledge*.[3] The theories expounded in that book seemed, to some colleagues, to be tainted with Lamarckism. Such a suggestion probably arose from the principal assertion which was insisted upon throughout: that there was an inherent improbability in ascribing extremely well-organized and extensive powers of synthesis to the genome itself, unless the many regulating forces involved supply it with "feedback" information as to the success or failure of endogenous developments. The earlier study was, however, lacking in precision; the present work is intended to provide this. It seems quite evident that the information feedbacks referred to need comprise no "message," properly so called. (There will therefore be no need to refer, in what follows, to the "reverse transcriptase" passing from RNA to DNA discovered by H. W. Temin and others.) Feedback need consist only in the progressive and retroactive repercus-

---

3. *Biology and Knowledge* (Chicago: The University of Chicago Press, 1971) — Trans.

sions (by selective obstruction or blocking) occasioned by a loss of equilibrium. In other words, the supposed message may consist of a *noncodified* indication that "something isn't working." When everything is functioning normally, on the other hand, there will be no need for any such indication. The point was made, in *Biology and Knowledge*,[4] that in fact Waddington had gone even further than I had in the direction for which I was subsequently reproached for want of the specifics put forward here.

It is hoped that the present study, which proposes a possible model for the replacement of exogenous by endogenous processes, will find wider acceptance for a writer who has been a tireless opponent of empiricism in the field of epistemology and consequently of pure Lamarckism in biology.

March 1973

J.P.

---

4. In a footnote to p. 400 of the new French edition (p. 294 in the English edition of 1971) — Trans.

Preliminaries

The term "phenocopy" is currently applied to an exogenous and nonhereditary (thus phenotypic) somatic modification, which imitates quite precisely the morphological characteristics of a true mutation or hereditary (genotypic) variation. There is, however, general agreement that the formation of this imitative adaptation precedes in time that of the corresponding mutation. The term "copy" of course, in its normal usage, is applied only to the reproduction of a preexisting model: it cannot be said of a precursor, for instance, that he has "copied" the work of a man who comes after him. The major problem posed by the phenocopy, then, is that of the "copying" of the phenotype by the genotype which succeeds it,[1] and not the copying by the phenotype of a mutation not yet produced (unless of course the phenotypic variation is considered a forerunner, already partly influenced by a genetic mechanism which develops subsequently).

Whatever the terminological difficulties, the problem of the phenocopy is of great theoretical interest. If the resemblance between the exogenous somatic modification and the corresponding mutation is not purely fortuitous (and the high frequency of the phenomenon would seem to preclude this), we have then to understand why it is that, as we believe rightly or wrongly, purely endogenous variations are able to converge with phenotypic modifications, the occurrence of which implies diverse degrees of environmental intervention.

Yet the first problem, of course, is that of knowing which has come first: the phenotypic variation or the new genotype? The phenocopy itself is only rarely observed under laboratory conditions, and it is difficult under natural conditions to establish the chronological sequence of events with any certainty. All that can usually be ascertained is that the exogenous somatic modification concerned is more widespread and frequent, whereas the hereditary modification appears only

1. This point is noted by, among others, Konrad Lorenz, writing of behavior patterns which become hereditary in certain species of ducks. Lorenz proposed the term "genocopy" for such a phenomenon. See *L'Agression,* Flammarion, 1969, pp. 72-73 (English edition, *On Aggression,* 1966).

at some more or less localized point. This suggests the hypothesis that the hereditary modification is formed later. This point can be illustrated by the example of
Sedum album L., a well-known member of the Crassulaceae. When growing at an
altitude of 2000 m or above, this plant always has diminutive stems, leaves, and
flowers. As the present writer has often verified, however, it regains its normal
size of growth when transplanted into a lowland habitat, beginning at about
1600 m. Such a change can only represent a nonhereditary adaptation to altitude.
On the other hand, descendants of a population of the same dwarf form found
growing on the summit of Môle (1900 m) in Haute-Savoie maintained their characteristic form, after removal to habitats in Geneva and the plain of Faucigny.
Consequently, it must belong to a neighbouring genotypic variety *(micranthum
Bast.)*. In this case it would seem very likely that the mutation has succeeded the
phenotypic modification, and not the reverse. To justify such a conclusion, however, as in all cases of exogenous modification, an extensive and detailed study
under natural conditions would be essential.

The development of the phenocopy is thus a potentially enormous subject, perhaps even more so than is often thought. For this reason, preparation for this
study has included observations of organisms in many different locations, over a
period of some years. These observations have concentrated upon the variations
shown by a Mediterranean species of *Sedum,* the *S. sediforme* (also known as
Nicaense or *altissimum*). In the process, a new hereditary variety was fortunately
discovered, on the northern margins of the species' range of distribution, and this
new type (variety *parvulum*) provides a good example of a phenocopy. Other observations had previously been made of the races and phenotypes of the aquatic
snail *Limnaea stagnalis,* which inhabits lakes and marshes. Detailed analyses of
these investigations will be combined as a basis of reference in the present en-
quiry. The study will be organized, briefly, as follows:

It seems best to begin (chapter 1) by showing clearly how a genotype is recognized under natural conditions and what the respective roles of the genome and the
environment are in the course of growth or epigenesis. In fact, genotypes are
always embodied in phenotypes (it is the same in the laboratory). The two kinds
of phenotype possible (which can also be seen as poles of a continuum) will then
be examined (chapter 2). These are distinguished by the extent of direct environmental influence on individual morphology.[2] In one this influence is indeed direct
(as in the modification of an organism's size by variation in the availability of
nutrients); in the other, environmental effects operate through the medium of innate and specialized regulating mechanisms (to modify, for instance, the skin-

---

2. Some regulating factors, of course, are always operative, but in cases of direct influence their
function is only very general.

pigmentation of a white man or the level of chlorophyll in a plant). Findings from the long-term observations of *Sedum* and *Limnaea* will then be summarized (chapter 3) from the standpoint of relevance to the phenocopy. Hypotheses which have already been put forward to account for the phenocopy and analogous processes will then be reviewed (chapter 4), and the explanatory model which this study proposes will be developed (chapter 5). This has the double aim of countering unfounded suppositions of Lamarckism and of transcending the rather simplistic schemata implicit in orthodox neo-Darwinism. The hypothesis presented being founded upon processes of regulation and equilibration, we shall conclude (in part II) with a comparison between these endogenous processes and those involved in elementary forms of behavior. This will bring us back, through new arguments, to the ideas developed earlier in *Biology and Knowledge*.

This scheme leads us, of course, towards problems of psychology and epistemology, and away from biology. It is comforting to note, however, that the same direction was taken by the discoverer of organic selection and the phenocopy: J. M. Baldwin, after his article of 1896 on the effect which now bears his name, went on to become a great psychologist.

Part I
The Biological Problems

1. Genotype and Epigenetic System

It should be recalled at the outset that there is neither simple opposition nor simple parallelism between the concepts of genotype and phenotype. This would be the case only if, after describing the observable characteristics of various phenotypes, one could achieve the same precision with the genotype in its pure state by direct measurement of individuals from a carefully selected strain. It is clear, on the one hand, that a phenotype is dependent at all times upon its genotype, and not only upon the environment. Yet a genotype, on the other hand, is always embodied in phenotypes. Even when it constitutes a pure strain (which is in any case never certain), its representatives inhabit a particular environment, natural or artifical, and are to varying degrees dependent upon it. A genotype must therefore be characterized, in the first place, by the features common to all its phenotypes in all their environments. Second, it must be descriptively differentiated from other genotypes developed contemporaneously in an identical environment.

It will be seen at once how this dual requirement must complicate the diagnosis of hereditary variations and simple phenotypic adaptations — and their distinction is, of course, fundamental to study of the phenocopy. A double experimental approach is consequently advisable. First, in order to distinguish between an indefinite number of genotypes, it is necessary to cultivate those varieties which one believes to be hereditary over several years (or a sufficient number of generations) under the same environmental conditions. In the case of *Sedum sediforme*, our study will be confined to three distinct varieties: *altissimum* (very tall and generally blue-green in color), *medium* (of moderate size and similar coloration), and *parvulum* (a green dwarf form). The characters of these varieties are effectively maintained even when they are grown in the same cultivation bed or the same plant pot. Second, however, it was necessary to repeat these experiments under varying environmental conditions.[1] The plants were therefore grown at various altitudes (400, 900, or 1600 m), in various soils, under various sunlight and shade

---

1. Carefully avoiding hybridization, however, which is very common in *Sedum*.

conditions, and so on — and parts of these cultures were transplanted, from time to time, from one environment to another. The formation of phenotypic modifications could therefore be ascertained, since they would not be stable under altered environmental conditions. For instance, a colony of *medium* may adopt the *parvulum* form under unfavorable conditions, but revert to *medium* type if a further change occurs. Similarly, *parvulum* plants may grow taller and present a *medium* adaptation if grown on well-fertilized garden compost. They will, however, return to the *parvulum* form in the same undisturbed plot when, after a year or so, rain has washed the fertilizer out of the soil — unless, of course, more fertilizer is added.

These complicated procedures demand a degree of patience, until the existence of distinct genotypes can be ascertained and their various phenotypic variations recognized. Patience is rewarded, however, from the theoretical viewpoint, in that we are shown the complexity of interactions between the environment and biochemical syntheses of growth controlled by the genetic program. These interactions raise the whole question of epigenesis, of what Waddington has called the "epigenetic system" and Mayr the "epigenotype."

In the first place, it should be remembered that we hardly ever — perhaps even never — find isolated genotypes under natural conditions. We find only populations: systems of interconnected genotypes subject to the possibility of panmixis. The fundamental unit is then no longer the genome characteristic of a genotype more or less isolable in the laboratory, but rather the genetic pool of the population as a system in the sense that it has its own regulating mechanisms, as was shown in the classic experiments of Dobzhansky and Spassky,[2] and consequently its own "genetic homeostasis." When we speak of the three hereditary varieties *altissimum, medium,* and *parvulum* as genotypes therefore, we make a strictly unwarranted extension of the term, legitimate only as convenient abbreviation. We should in fact almost certainly speak in terms of genetic pools and populations. These populations are thus only represented by individuals with apparently stable hereditary characteristics. Each has its own complex genome which is only a partial image of the genetic pool of the population concerned.

Having said that, we should consider a question fundamental to any interpretation of the phenocopy: that of the part played by environmental influences during epigenesis. It is widely known, of course, that every genome, simple or complex, performs two very basic functions. On the one hand it ensures the hereditary transmission of the information contained in its DNA, and thus determines the

_____

2. These writers raised a mixed assembly of fourteen distinct races in a "population cage." After a phase of disequilibrium, they found that equilibrium was progressively restored, and that factors formerly operative were largely reestablished. Populations come to possess, in addition, their own adaptive norms, genetic recombinations being more prevalent than simple mutations; and it will be evident from this that an essential part is played by the multiple heterozygotes.

characteristics of subsequent generations. On the other hand, it imposes a constant structure on the individual organism during its growth: through the medium of RNA, etc., it ensures protein-synthesis according to an innate program which is ultimately that of its DNA. This process is directed centrifugally, but minute adjustments must take place at every developmental level (germ-cell, intercellular connections, tissues, and organs). These adjustments require the operation of a great number of very delicate regulating mechanisms, particularly those of allosteric nature[3] — and they imply the constant collaboration of all genes in a concerted operation.

What, then, is the part played by the environment during these successive syntheses and their complex regulation? Some writers merely insist upon the importance of its role in nutrition: the growing organism must, after all, be capable of integrating the substances and energies necessary to its development. This integrative process might therefore be understood as merely assimilation of external contributions to endogenous structures imposed by the genetic program, without any concomitant structural alteration. If that were so, then the system's equilibrium could be interpreted as nothing more than the result of complete predetermination. Certainly there would be continuous construction. There could, therefore, be no return to the tenets of static preformism, held by partisans of sperm and egg before P. J. Wolff's discovery rendered the doctrine obsolete. But this construction would still conform to a genetic program which remains, in itself, preformed. This would mean development that could not be modified by external events.

Simple observation should be sufficient to show us that the opposite is true. The inevitable environmental disturbances which occur during epigenesis are in fact quite capable of being translated into significant morphological modifications. One instance of this is provided by a variation in the shell of *Limnaea stagnalis*. This is a good example in that the operative factors are essentially mechanical, but the tissues are also involved, since the shell is secreted by the epidermis according to a design which is generally constant. This *Limnaea* develops an elongated form in pond habitats (fig. 1). In the more turbulent conditions of larger lakes, however, a variety *lacustris* is known to develop, the form of which is considerably more compact (fig. 2). The mechanism responsible for this variation, insofar as it is a simple phenotypic adaptation, will be described in chapter 2. During the growth of this *lacustris* variant, which is our only concern for the moment, it may happen that the creature's environment is significantly changed. Individuals originating in turbulent lake habitats may be removed to complete their development in the aquarium — or, if the level of the lake were to fall, an individual might complete the construction of its shell in the very different conditions of a pool left isolated

---

3. Through mediators ensuring spatial adjustment.

FIGURE 1
Limnaea subula.

FIGURE 2
Limnaea lacustris.

FIGURE 3
Result of change in environment during growth of *lacustris* phenotype.

above the new waterline. In these two instances there would follow a quite remarkable change in the form of the shell. Half of it would develop in the shorter,
compact form, this being a phenotypic modification in imitation of the hereditary
variety *lacustris* (fig. 3). The other half would show a reversion to the normal
elongated shape of still water varieties.

Such a phenomenon, while confirming the constraining role of the hereditary programming of the elongated varieties, shows at the same time that, during one phase of epigenesis, the environment has in itself exerted a very important morphogenetic influence by imposing the "shorter shell" phenotypic variation. For the present, this environmental influence during epigenesis should simply be noted, without prejudging in any way the explanation of how the hereditary varieties of *lacustris* are formed. The environment has here induced an effect which, while to an extent remaining subject to the hereditary program, was not foreseen by it. We can thus speak here, without exaggeration, of interaction. On the one hand the effect of the genetic program has certainly been modified by the changed environment. On the other, the environmental effect has itself been conditioned by the limits imposed by the hereditary programming upon the range of possible variations. Observations of *Sedum* provide another example. Some whole plants were noted whose branches had apparently begun their growth in the *medium* form (leaves averaging 8-10 mm in length and only slightly convex). Their development had been completed, however, in the *parvulum* form (leaves 5-6 mm long, with a pronounced underside convexity). The resulting branches (5-8 cm in length) showed a clear discontinuity between these growth forms. This modification might arise in response to climatic variation (drought after a period of wet weather, or the reverse), or to variation in light of terrain, etc. Whatever the ultimate cause, transplantation from one location to another has in this case produced a discontinuous alteration of growth, in the shape as well as the size of leaves. These modifications, again, were not foreseen in the innate genetic program, and must therefore be due to environmental factors.

There remains a most important question concerning the nature of the genotype and the part it plays in the course of epigenesis. On the one hand, are these environmental effects upon epigenetic development to be taken as simply unfortunate or inconsequential accidents? Is the power of producing these phenotypic adaptations, on the other hand, indicative of a certain dynamism? In the latter case, such a capability would be extremely useful, in that a greater flexibility would undoubtedly be advantageous to the survival and continued propagation of the genotype concerned. To this second question, however, J. Monod would certainly give a negative answer. Evolution itself, in his opinion, insofar as it involves the production of new genotypes, is "in no way a property of living creatures since it is rooted in the very imperfections of that preservation mechanism which is uniquely their advantage."[4] With good reason, then, the necessity of undergoing all kinds of phenotypic modifications under environmental influence might seem ascribable

---

4. [nullement une propriété des êtres vivants, puisqu'elle a sa racine dans les imperfections mêmes du mécanisme conservateur qui, lui, constitue bien leur unique privilège.] *Le hasard et la nécessité* (1970), p. 130.

to "imperfections" even more unfortunate. Dobzhansky, Waddington, and others take the contrary view, seeing these phenotypes as the genotype's responses to the stresses or hostility of the environment. This term "response," however, with its suggestion of activity must be considered in greater detail.

To allow that environmental agencies, exerting their visible effects on the production of phenotypic variations, may have had repercussions extending to the genome — and that the response referred to may arise directly from this — would surely be out of the question. Acceptance of such a hypothesis would involve a virtual return to Lamarckism. It would imply that the environment had produced immediate modification of this genome — not only instigating an accommodative response, but also allowing the possibility that the response might become hereditarily fixed. And this, of course, might as well be called the transmission of an acquired characteristic, in the Lamarckian sense of those words. Since there has never been experimental verification of such a phenomenon, the only remaining possibility is to interpret both the environmental action and the "response" of the genome as occurring at a particuler stage of epigenetic development. Genetic information passes from DNA to RNA to control the initial selection of amino acids from which proteins are synthesized. Between the starting point of this genetic message and its outcome will be the vast process of epigenetic construction by which the organism attains its adult state. Between origin and culmination there exists, of course, a number of hierarchical levels comparable to relays of one sort or another. Each step of the construction will be characterized by successive processes of synthesis, all evidently directed by genetic information. Since growth, however, involves the continual assimilation of contributions from outside the system, the part played by the environment will be all the more important as the higher stages of development are approached. This will lead to one of two possible results. External factors of nutrition may have no modifying effect at all upon these progressive developments, in which case they will be completed, without deviation, according to the hereditary program. Alternatively, there may be divergence or opposition between the exogenous factors in the environment and the endogenous processes of development. It is then that these endogenous processes will react. Since they are directed by the genome, the reaction they produce at the level of epigenesis concerned can then fittingly be termed a "response of the genome."

But of what does this genomic response consist? Any of the stages of development just outlined will be characterized by a system of regulations or of causal loops in which every stage is dependent on its predecessors and controls its successors. It is necessary, however, that on the level considered the reactions involved form a system which is both open and at the same time closed in a cycle.[5] In an extreme-

5. Cf. the *intégrons* invoked by F. Jacob.

ly generalized and simplified form, this might be expressed as follows: $(A \times A' \to C)$... $(Y \times Y' \to B)$, $(B \times B' \to Z)$, $(Z \times Z' \to A)$, where A', B'... Y', Z' are external aliments, and A, B, C... Z, A are elements of the cyclic system itself.

Still generalizing excessively but necessarily, the response of the genome, or more accurately of the synthetic apparatus it directs, will be restricted to two possibilities. Environmental change (symbolized by alteration of A' to A'' or B' to B'', etc.) may end by destroying the cycle, in which case growth is obstructed and the organism will consequently die. The environmental action may, alternatively, prove acceptable, in which case the closing of the cyclic system remains possible, on condition that another local alteration takes place. (For instance, the exogenous alteration of A' to A'' would lead to the modification of A into $A2$; but $A2 \times A''$ would continue to give B, other parts of the system remaining unchanged.) The endogenous response, in other words, if it is positive, certainly constitutes an accomodation of the system to the new environmental situation — but one which maximally conserves its cyclic coherence. There is one sense in which this response is conservative or even restrictive: it excludes unacceptable variations, and preserves (by a kind of optimization) all that can be retained from "normal" processes of synthesis. Yet in another sense the response is dynamic and even innovative, since it ensures adjustement of the old system to new and unforeseen circumstances.

It should be emphasized, however, that this tentative interpretation of the genome's accommodatory responses in no way concerns the problem of heredity to which we will return in chapter 2. Reactions taking place at the higher stages of epigenetic synthesis do not, in fact, necessarily modify what happens at lower levels of development. These genomic responses are only phenotypic, which means, on the contrary, that once the prevailing environmental influence (resulting from the alteration of A' to A'') is suppressed, the accommodatory response (changing A into $A2$) also comes to an end. The former cycle $(A \times A' \to B'$, etc.) will then immediately reestablish itself, and regain its former equilibrium. There is thus no question, in this hypothesis, of acquired characteristics being hereditarily fixed or transmitted.

If the ideas broadly outlined here are acceptable, it follows that the greater the number of phenotypic responses available to any genotype, the greater its advantage. Indeed, this plasticity will be a measure of its vitality. A very relevant suggestion is made by P. P. Grassé in a stimulating article[6] concerning the lowland plant species subjected to alpine conditions by Bonnier. These plants developed somatic modifications characteristic of plants found on alpine facies, but these did not prove to be hereditary when they were returned to normal habitats. Grassé

---

6. In *Savoir et action* (November, 1972).

argues that this flexibility was more useful to these plants than the formation of new genotypes which might have been overspecialized. This is perhaps to take the idea too far, but it does seem certain that, from the point of view of adaptation and preadaptation, a genotype with multiple phenotypes would be at a definite advantage. For example, in a study undertaken years ago of several species of terrestrial mollusks widespread in Valais, we established a positive correlation between the size variation of these species in lowland, and the altitude at which they were able to live in their smaller forms.[7] In this case, therefore, the number of distinct phenotypes available initially constitutes a factor in possible adaptation to mountainous terrain.

This leads us to the problem of norms of reaction. It is known that, in terms of the values $V1... Vn$ of a particular environmental variable, a genotype can react by adopting the characteristic forms $F1... Fn$, these being the given genotype's possible phenotypic variations in relation to this variable. Such a "norm of reaction" is especially interesting from the viewpoint of the limits tolerated by the genotype concerned. These limits can only be transgressed when new variations or genetic combinations are initiated, which will in turn set up new norms, distinct from the former ones. In this connection there are, however, two points which should be noted. One is that the norm of reaction, though helping to explain interactions between epigenetic processes and environment as has just been considered, in no way permits us to distinguish the precise border between the effects of exogenous and endogenous factors in the phenotypes concerned. We only know that both kinds of factor are at work: the former because nonhereditary modifications occur, the latter because they are limited. Yet the precise boundary between the two spheres of influence remains indeterminate. The second point is that though norms of reaction with one or two environmental variables are easily constructed, the total combination of possible conditions is never known. Nor, as a consequence, can one know all the phenotypes which might potentially arise, even though they have yet to be observed. Whence arises, of course, the great difficulty of identifying or characterizing genotypes under natural conditions.

The foregoing remarks would tend to indicate that two antagonistic forces or tendencies are at work in the heart of the epigenetic system. These were pointed out as significant from the outset, since their equilibrium or lack of it plays a most important part in the formation, or lack of formation, of phenocopies. The first of these two tendencies is naturally conservative. In the course of the successive syntheses ensured by the genome, this tendency compels development to abide by the genetic program, to follow the "necessary paths" or "chreods" of which

7. J. Piaget, Corrélation entre la répartition verticale des mollusques du Valais et les indices de variations spécifiques [Correlation between the vertical distribution of the mollusks of Valais and indices of species variation], Revue suisse de zoologie 28 (1920) : 125-153.

Waddington speaks. It also compels the synthetic processes to cancel or compensate any deviation, by means of a stabilizing mechanism bearing on the trajectories, and resulting, therefore, in "homeorhesis" rather than simply homeostasis. The second force at work in the epigenetic system is one which also demands very careful attention. In no way is it simply an inverse tendency towards variation — that would be absurd. Rather, it encourages a kind of selective flexibility, making modifications imposed by the environment more or less acceptable according to circumstances. As a result, the processes by which the norm of reaction is reestablished are very complex. For instance, there will obviously be a great difference in the degree of acceptability to the epigenetic program between somatic modifications due to the etiolation of a plant and simple variations in its size. In the former instance, a *Sedum* half-choked and deprived of light by surrounding weeds of greater height can nevertheless live on for weeks or months, and regain its normal form once the ground is cleared. In such a case, modification takes the form of very long, thin stems: leaves are widely spaced on the stem, and the whole plant is very pale in color. Accommodations have clearly occurred which are necessary to current conditions, but which are in no sense desirable. On the other hand, more commonly occurring variations in its size are of much more lasting use to the plant. They allow adjustments between its surface area and volume, which are of value in relating parts of the plant engaged in its nutrition with the mass requiring sustenance. Such modifications are thus responsive both to environmental conditions and to the requirements of synthesis, a hereditary program allowing considerable margins in its realization, since it must take account of many very variable factors.

To summarize: A genotype's norm of reaction would certainly seem to depend upon, among other factors, a compromise between two tendencies. These are quite distinct and, in a sense, mutually opposed. One is conservative, acting against potentially harmful environmental modifications which might endanger equilibrium. The other is a tendency towards flexibility. It aims to utilize exogenous modifications within those limits where their contribution will be advantageous, even though the effect of their multiple combinations cannot be foreseen. This also, however, raises a great problem: that of the kinds of equilibration achieved by phenotypes. This problem is, moreover, quite liable to reappear in different forms where the formation of hereditary modifications is concerned. Phenotypic equilibration might, on the one hand, constitute a simple return after accommodation to the preceding form of equilibrium or another analogous form. It might, on the other hand, be accompanied by some kind of optimizing effect. In other words, the form of equilibrium pursued would then be the best that could be attained under the given conditions.

2. The Complexity of Phenotypes

The foregoing remarks on epigenesis and norms of reaction provide us with one immediate conclusion: the problem of exogenous somatic modification of the phenotype is both much more complex and more interesting than has often been supposed. Because a phenotypic adaptation is the product of environmental influences, and because the effects of such exogenous processes are not hereditarily transmitted, it has often been too swiftly concluded that the mechanism of phenotypic variation has no bearing on the theory of evolutionary change. In fact, however, an understanding of events at any stage of modification can only teach us more (by contrast as well as analogy) about the mechanisms which are distinctively operational at other levels.

The first point of interest and the first specific lesson to be drawn from an examination of phenotypic modifications is that such modifications are by no means confined to a single form, as if all had occurred at the same stage of epigenetic development. Quite the opposite is true, and a very careful distinction must be made between modifications at the higher level, that of the form of organs, which may frequently be further complicated by the intrusion of behavioral factors (in the guise of acquired and noninnate habits), modifications at the level of tissue morphology, and modifications at the level of intercellular connection, etc. There exists, in short, a whole range of nonhereditary variations. Those of the higher levels exhibit maximal influence of the environment at grips with an innate program. These modifications are of an inclusive nature such as the morphogenesis of one organ or another. At elementary levels variation is more and more subject to hereditary regulators, the environment's actions tending to be reduced to setting something going rather than constituting oriented directives.

This, however, is only the first essential dimension in the classification of nonhereditary modifications. A second dimension demands separate consideration since it is of undoubted significance to any discussion of the problem of phenocopies. The question is that of the degree of stability attained by the phenotype, insofar as it does achieve more or less stable accommodations. This question carries a quite precise significance in the case of *Sedum*, entire colonies of which are able to reproduce by vegetative means for years at a time, arising, therefore, from the same genetic generation but developing multiple somatic modifications of exterior origin. Thus the question of the nature of phenotypic equilibrium, indicated above, is raised once more. To what extent is this merely a matter of simple conservation involving a return to the former state at the time that environmental disturbances are neutralized? Or is it to be understood as a process of equilibration, involving optimization (or at least improvement), in other words, realization of a better form of equilibrium? Obviously, such questions as these will have an evident bearing on the more general problem which faces us — that of the phenocopy. There is the fact, for instance, that a phenotypic adaptation may be replaced at any given time by a genotype composed of analogous (or at least apparently analogous) characteristics. Such replacement must depend partly upon the more or less stable properties of the initial phenotypic modification, and upon the extent to which its values approach the optimum. The reasons for such possible dependence are still, of course, to be discovered. Does it follow, for example, merely because a phenotype is stable and is reproduced unchanged with each new generation — e.g., the contracted forms of a species of hereditarily elongated *Limnaea* — that the chances of its being succeeded by an identical form of genotype will be greater? Or, on the contrary, when a phenotypic variation is stable and, moreover, advantageous from the point of view of optimization, will there be less probability of a phenocopy being produced by a new genotype, since phenotypic adaptation already meets every requirement? At the level of conduct, for example, phenotypic acquisition, i.e., learning of the mother tongue by successive generations, would seem optimal as compared to hereditary fixation of a particular language. Moreover, no language has ever been fixed in humans by hereditary processes. It seems self-evident, therefore, that this second solution is the more probable. Unfortunately, neither the degree of phenotypic equilibrium nor its approach to the optimum can currently be verifiably determined, and the possible interdependence of these factors and the production of a phenocopy is still more obscure. Yet this is no reason for abandoning an attempt to clarify such problems, or for discounting those facts which appear significant.

(I A) Phenotypes may be classified according to the level of epigenetic development at which the environment comes into conflict with genetic programming. On this basis the first level to be considered is the most inclusive or externally oriented as it concerns only the morphology of organs. To return to the example of the still water or lacustrine *Limnaea*, the organ in question will be the shell or test, which is secreted by the epidermis during the course of growth. On its emergence from the egg, the creature as yet has only one-and-a-half whorls, whereas in the adult state the spiral will comprise about seven turns. The construction of this testaceous covering is, however, minutely controlled by genetic information, since it strictly differentiates one species from another. Thus *Limnaea stagnalis* has a very elongated shell, with a long, pointed spiral; the shell of *Limnaea palustris* is even more elongated but less sharply pointed. On the other hand, *Limnaea auricularia, L. ovata,* and *L. peregra* all have shorter, more compact shell forms, the first of these three being particularly squat, with a short spiral and a very large aperture. In marshes, ponds, and waterways, *Limnaea stagnalis* develops several variants of its normal elongated form. When individuals are reared under identical conditions in the aquarium, three known hereditary varieties or genotypes can be identified as follows: variety 1, *subula,* a particularly slender form (fig. 1); variety 2, which corresponds to the most frequently occurring type of the species; and variety 3, *turgida,* a shorter, thicker form which generally lives on the mud of small ponds or pools. These three varieties are found in the calm waters of larger lakes, or in bays where there is sufficient plant life (pondweed, etc.) for the *Limnaea* to live on without growth problems. Variety 3, however, and occasionally variety 2, may select habitats where conditions are very different. Where shallow waters are made turbulent by wind or waves, where there is little or no aquatic vegetation and the bottom is a gentle gradient of stones, both these varieties show adaptation to a very much shortened form. That such variations are certainly phenotypic can be shown by the rearing of their descendants in controlled aquarium conditions. It is shown also by the relatively abrupt changes of form which follow environmental alteration during growth (chapter 1, fig. 3). We are thus not yet dealing with *lacustris* genotypes, which will be considered in chapter 3, but only with nonhereditary somatic forms.

Their formation is easy enough to explain. Throughout its development — between the construction of the first and seventh whorls of its shell — the animal must withstand rough conditions when they arise. To do this, it must adhere securely to the rock or stone on which it happens to be. This is easily achieved by means of a muscular "foot," developing a suction power which is generally quite strong (as in the case of the marine *Patellae,* which resist much more powerful forces). This attachment, however, involves two simultaneous consequences. In the first place, the growing *Limnaea* exerts a ceaseless drag upon its columellar muscle, that is, the muscle which attaches it to its shell, being anchored on the columella or axis of the spiral. As a consequence, the shell's formation is constantly subject to effects of traction which tend to shorten it. Second, with each pressing of the shell against its rocky anchorage, there is some expansion of its aperture. The combination of these two effects, shortening of the spiral and enlargement of the aperture, will profoundly modify the overall shape of the shell, which tends to become squat and globular. This process might well be described as "patellization," in the sense of a suppression of the spiral, and development of a cowled shape with a large aperture.

It is clear that in such phenotypes as these the hereditary program, which prescribes the morphology of the creature's protective organ (its shell), is quite substantially modified. The agents of this modification are the mechanical action of the environment (disturbance of the water), and the equally mechanical response of the creature itself (traction or contraction of a muscle and pressure of the shell aperture against its anchorage). It is important to recognize, in addition, that these adaptive responses of the animal are not exclusively physiological, but in large part arise from its behavior. On the one hand, the application of the suction foot to the stone is a reflex. On the other hand, however, there is a factor of habit which reinforces the action. Marsh-dwelling individuals of this same species *stagnalis*, which possess the same reflex, in fact make very little use of it according to aquarium observations. If shaken about, they most frequently react by detaching themselves from their anchorage and allowing themselves to sink to the muddy bottom. This second course of behavior would generally be fatal to lake-dwelling individuals: fracturing of the shell would entail considerable damage to flesh and internal organs. It is thus a striking observation that, placed in an aquarium, phenotypes gathered from a lake habitat will only very rarely react in this way. To the morphological phenotype, there is thus added an acquired behavior pattern (systematic choice of reaction) which is therefore equally a phenotypic characteristic. More follows, however. When, as here, a phenotypic variation involves both the form of an organ and behavior, the part played by the environment cannot be considered essentially disruptive. We face, on the contrary, one of those situations in which the organism chooses its environment — and chooses it, in this particular case, in a doubly active fashion. In the first place, nothing obliges it to leave a habitat in marshes or placid lake inlets in order to anchor itself on a more exposed shore. In the second place, nothing forces it to survive under such conditions instead of taking shelter in the sublittoral zone — where, in fact, the variety *Bollingeri*[1] maintains an elongated form (although small) in calm waters at depths of 10-30 m. There is here, then, an important finding from the standpoint of an equilibration aimed at improvement. For here the accommodative response comprises, in addition to its compensatory effects, an unquestionable gain in the form of an extension of the environment and an enhanced adaptability.

For the present, we remain on the subject of the analysis of phenotypes. The time has not yet come to discuss the one or more corresponding genotypes constituted

---

1. *Bollingeri* Piaget, a new variety reported in the present writer's study, Les mollusques sublittoraux du Léman [The Sublittoral mollusks of Lake Geneva], *Zoologischer Anzeiger* 42 (1913): 619-24.

by the varieties *lacustris* and *bodamica* (see chapter 3) in the beautiful example of the phenocopy provided by the *Limnaea stagnalis* in its adaptation to life in lakes.

(I B) Turning to phenotypes which arise at the level of tissues as well as organs, examples of these will include variations in size. Of interest here are the regulations or equilibrations involved in exchanges or interactions between environmental factors and the working out of the hereditary program of the epigenetic syntheses. For example, there are the well-known rules laid down by Bergmann and Allen, which govern increase in the size of animals relative to a lowering of temperatures. This effect is explained as a modification which diminishes surface area in proportion to volume, thus allowing economy in transpiration. According to Hovasse, this modification of a creature's size would in itself be "primitively phenotypic."[2] In plants, on the contrary, a diminution in size is observed when environmental conditions are unfavorable, as, for instance, when growth occurs above certain altitudes. This particularly concerns us, of course, in relation to *Sedum*. One factor involved in this stunting effect is undoubtedly the increase in ultraviolet radiation at high altitudes. In general, however, the effect of an increase in surface area relative to volume is to increase the efficiency of alimentation (of chlorophyll assimilation by leaves and of moisture absorption by roots). At the same time, of course, the volume of tissue to be nourished is reduced. It is generally believed, especially in unfavorable situations (irrespective of altitude), that such modifications will be phenotypic. It has also been shown, following the well-known experiments of G. Bonnier, that the alpine adaptations of species transplanted to mountain habitats will remain nonhereditary in nature.

In the case of *Sedum*, such dwarf phenotypes are continually apparent. Those of *Sedum album* have been mentioned in chapter 1, and we will return in chapter 3 to those of *S. sediforme*. Conversely, it has been noted that on temporarily fertilized soil very large phenotypes develop, which then revert to a more normal height once this brief fertility is exhausted. Such findings are of course quite commonplace, but they must be recalled when we come to discuss, in chapter 3, the status of the phenocopy in the hereditary variety *parvulum*.

By contrast, a quite curious phenotypic variation, also involving size, is that shown by some aquatic mollusks in relation to the size of the aquariums (or even of the ponds) in which they live. Countless specimens of varieties 1-5 of *Limnaea stagnalis*, reared in one-liter aquariums, all remained much reduced in size. In larger tanks, on the other hand, their size increased. This variation seems to occur equally in relation to the extent of the small pools in which they are found under natural conditions. The present writer has been able to verify this on many occa-

---

2. "primitivement phénotypique" (*Biologie* volume of the *Encyclopédie de la Pléiade*, p. 1679).

sions, especially when cultures were placed in a small pond which subsequently became even smaller. This factor of the extent of the habitat is clearly of some importance: the quantity of food available — easily controlled in the aquarium — does not in fact seem to be the dominant environmental consideration. This would suggest that in this case, as with variation in the shell form itself, behavioral factors play some part, sufficient space for movement or exercise being essential for normal growth and development.

(I C) As interactions between the environment and epigenetic development come nearer to the level of intercellular connections, so the part played by exogenous factors in the production of phenotypes is progressively less formative. Such factors are increasingly restricted to the role of triggering mechanisms, or to that of inhibiting developments already envisaged in the hereditary program. The incidence of skin pigmentation in response to solar radiation is a case in point. It is not sunlight which directly produces the melanic screen in the epidermal cells, in the same way that water turbulence produces the effect of contraction in the shell of *Limnaea*. The melanin and its regulation arise rather from the functioning of a preestablished system, which environmental influence will merely activate. In the same way, the abrasion which produces callouses in man does not directly produce the similarly epidermal response of keratinization: it only triggers its activation, which is not at all the same thing.

In the case of *Sedum sediforme,* while the type of the species is blue-green in color, the usual forms of the variety *parvulum* (and also of the diminutive phenotypes which imitate it) are a more or less darker green. My colleague, the botanist Grépin, has been kind enough to demonstrate that, for plants of equal size, green specimens possess more chlorophyll and show evidence of greater powers of photosynthesis.[3] The following observations should then perhaps prove instructive: whereas the typical *S. sediforme* of southern France is indifferent to frost, blue-green examples from the Balearic Islands (Ibiza) froze when grown in Geneva. Only a few branches recovered, and they then produced new leaves which were green. This transition from blue-green to green is observed among small sized specimens and among those partially deprived of light, for instance in woods northward from Tibidabe to Barcelona, as well as when growth recovers after frost. It seems to be evidence of compensatory reaction to adverse circumstances. Here again, however, it is a question of environmental activation of mechanisms which, in their structure and regulation, are genetically preordained. There is no new formation under the direct influence of exogenous factors.

---

3. With some reservation in respect of the age of branches, but for practical purposes this was the same.

It can therefore be stated, all evidence considered, that there exist distinct forms of phenotype or phenotypic response corresponding to different levels of epigenetic development. At higher levels (organ morphology for instance), where genetically controlled processes of development must respond with maximal flexibility or adaptability, environmental actions have the greatest formative influence. As more elementary levels of development are approached, on the other hand, interaction will be increasingly dominated by the hereditary program and its regulating effects: the role of the environment is then reduced, at the limit, to acting only as a triggering agent. This is particularly the case when occasional accidental accommodations occur, as in instances of scarring or of local regeneration.

(II A) These distinctions between the various kinds of phenotypic reaction are of fundamental importance from the standpoint of equilibration. In broad terms, two forms of equilibrium should be brought into consideration. The first form is predominant at higher levels of epigenesis. The second is attained principally at the initial, more elementary levels of development, but can in fact be found at any stage of the process. The first form, again, is that which concerns relations between the external environment and the developmental syntheses of epigenesis. Thus in the case of lacustrine varieties of *Limnaea*, phenotypic equilibrium is attained when the degree of water turbulence is matched by the degree of shell contraction which permits the animal a sufficiently secure anchorage.

There exists, however, a second factor in such equilibration, which concerns the interrelationships of the levels of synthesis involved. On the one hand, each level, naturally, has its own mechanisms of regulation: whether relating to intra- or intercellular reactions, tissue development, or the morphogenesis of particular organs, each stage of development has its own peculiar controls. On the other hand, it is necessary for another form of equilibrium to be maintained. If epigenesis is to proceed without accidents, an equilibrium must be constantly preserved between each given level's regulating processes and those of levels above and below it. Hence this second form of equilibrium: in order that a phenotype may be formed, and thus be acceptable in terms of its genotype's norm of reaction, it is necessary that the accomodatory modification concerned attain equilibrium. This applies not only in relation to the endogenous synthesis of the level concerned, but also in relation to the collective and mutual interregulations which connect the different levels to each other.

The processes by which these two kinds of equilibrium are attained are themselves two-fold. On one hand they consist of *trials*, of gropings, within the limits of possible variation, and these tentative departures will be the source of new modifications characterizing the as yet unrealized phenotype. On the other hand, processes of *selection* are involved, which sanction the success or failure of the proposed modifications. In short, modification and selection will continually succeed each other, as is the case when any biological innovation occurs. Here, however, only nonhereditary variations are concerned.

The origin of the trial-variations referred to will differ according to the level. We have seen already (in I A above) that at the higher levels the source may even be fundamentally behavioral. At the level of the modification of an organ the example given was that of the shell of *Limnaea*. The animal responded actively to disturbance in its chosen environment. At more elementary levels, the trials occur relative to a kind of flexibility in genetic regulation when processes of epigenetic synthesis run up against some particular disequilibrium. Here, of course, there is still no question of new genetic variations or mutations. As for the processes of selection involved, a significant distinction must be drawn, resulting from that between the two kinds of equilibrium described above. The first equilibrium noted was that between the accommodatory modification and the influence of the surrounding environment. In this case, processes of selection will be employed which are charged with retaining successful trial-variations and discarding failures. Such selection will be that usually referred to as "external," since its operative factors derive ultimately from the external environment. The second kind of equilibrium, that between new or trial-variations and the epigenetic system of interregulations, involves another type of selection. This is usually known, by Baldwin's term, as organic selection. Here the selective factors concerned derive not only from these endogenous processes of regulation, but also from the internal environment as a whole, to which, of course, their functioning is liable.

We discussed, at the end of chapter 1, the two fundamental tendencies discernible in epigenesis. One was seen as strictly conservative, recognizable by the fact that reequilibration after environmental disturbance consists simply in a return to the former equilibrium. The other was distinguished by its adaptive flexibility, involving even optimization, and aiming if not at improvement, then at least at attaining the best equilibrium compatible with prevailing conditions. By recalling this, we can now draw conclusions as follows, regarding phenotypes and their different levels of formation. At higher developmental levels, the part played by behavior is of no small significance. This behavioral element, as has been seen in the phenotypic variations of *Limnaea,* is by no means confined to compensations in response to the perturbations or hostility of the environment. It may, on the contrary, take the form of behavior patterns designed to overcome difficulties, with a view to extension of a hitherto normal environment. Such behavior, where it occurs, involves exploitation of possible variations, and sometimes a broadening of the norm of reaction. Lacustrine phenotypes of *Limnaea* will, for example, go beyond the limits shown by still water phenotypes in their development of the shorter shell adaptation.

At intermediate developmental levels, it is clear that the principal function of the phenotype will be to respond to exogenous disturbances by means of accommodations which will vary according to the circumstances. The exogenous modifications in size and coloration shown by *Sedum* have been mentioned as a case in point. Here, however, detailed study of the whole range of nonhereditary variations — a type of analysis too much neglected by specialists in pure genetics — has revealed the existence of so many other phenotypes, that it is difficult not to interpret them as local improvements rather than as necessary reactions. The range of variation is clearly very wide, even if the general size of the plant (obviously dependent on such factors as nutrition, and conditions of light, temperature, and soil) is left out of account. Thus, wherever in the world the plant is found, and even in closely adjacent plots, tremendous variety can be observed. Some groups of individuals will have proportionally shortened or lengthened secondary branches: these may bear leaves throughout their length, or be ninetenths bare with a luxuriant tuft of foliage at the tip. The general form of the plant may be upright or may, alternatively, hug the ground, its stems creeping over the soil surface. The leaves may be deciduous, with an abundance of normal regrowth in spring, or again, they may survive throughout the winter months. And such a list of variations could well be continued. Indeed, our inevitable lack of information makes it impossible to draw a definite boundary among these features between what is imposed by a determinism acting in one direction and what represents only exploitation of a range of possible variations. In a partly open system, however, there are good theoretical grounds for believing that the set of its potential noncompensated transformations will play a fundamental part. The equilibrium of such a system is a matter of the mutual conservation of its parts, and not a matter of minimal potential energy as would be the case in a static physical state. This may very well explain that flexibility which is discernible over and above the more evident tendencies towards conservation.

The formation of hereditary variations remains to be discussed (chapter 5). If the foregoing arguments are acceptable, then the parallel question will inevitably arise (as it does at present for many writers): is the production of mutations entirely a matter of chance? Does it, on the other hand, occur as a kind of scanning procedure, exploring regions where a disequilibrium becomes apparent in the midst of a system as well-integrated as that of intracellular interactions?

For the present, however, there is the basic problem already mentioned, of how the different forms of equilibrium peculiar to phenotypes are related to the development of phenocopies. It should from now on be apparent what the hypothesis put forward here will be, and it may be stated as follows: where a phenotype has attained an optimal equilibrium between environmental influences and endogenous processes of regulation (including the interregulations which characterize epigenetic syntheses), the formation of phenocopies by new genotypes will be rendered pointless. On the other hand, however, a phenotype which allows the continued existence of internal disequilibrium, particularly those corresponding to the second type of equilibrium noted above, cannot but open the way for genotypic variations to occur. These will be directed into regions where there is malfunction of the system, and where scanning, with organic or internal selection, will resolve problems that the phenotype itself has not entirely been able to solve.

3. Summary Analysis
of Some Observational Data

At this stage, we should outline the observations which justify us in speaking of a phenocopy in the given instances of *Limnaea stagnalis* and *Sedum sediforme*. Two factual points remain to be resolved in this chapter, independently of those questions of interpretation which will occupy us in chapters 4 and 5. The first concerns the similarities or differences between the genotypes under consideration (hereditary varieties of these species of *Limnaea* and *Sedum*) and the corresponding phenotypes. The second is the question of the chronological precedence of their formation.

(I A) This last question should perhaps be discussed first. In the case of the *Limnaea*, it seems clear enough that shortened shell phenotypes are initially formed in relation to the genotypes *lacustris* (variety 4) and *bodamica* (variety 5). We have found these genotypes only on wind-exposed, gently sloping shores, in Lakes Constance (Bodan), Neufchâtel, and Geneva. The still water varieties (1-3) can in fact live in large lakes, either in placid inlets or on exposed shorelines, but only where there are no gently shelving beaches. They require a shore where the water deepens rapidly, and where the surface is well provided with the water plants amid which they live. It is for this reason that the most elongated form (the variety known as *subula*) lives in the Italian lakes. It is also found, interestingly, in a subfossil state, in the lacustrine chalk around La Tène, in locations which are occupied today by gentle, pebbled shores, with populations of *lacustris* and of shortened shell phenotypes. Everything would seem to indicate, therefore, that the colonization of the lakes by *Limnaea stagnalis* began with a phase during which the normal varieties (1-3) adopted habitats most like those of ponds or marshes. They then spread into initially much less favorable situations, or even, in exceptional circumstances (as at La Tène) had to survive environmental changes in their original positions. The present distribution of the species in these lakes is therefore as follows: (1) varieties 1-3 are found, without appreciable change, in calm waters or where aquatic plant life is abundant; (2) varieties *lacustris* (4) and *bodamica* (5) are localized exclusively on gently sloping pebbled shores exposed to wind and waves; (3) in intermediate zones between these two extremes a mixed population can be found. Genotypes 4 and 5 occur with phenotypes of variety 2 or, more especially, variety 3. It is generally impossible to distinguish these phenotypes from the genotypes, except by rearing their immediate descendants in the aquarium; (4) finally, in the sublittoral zone, there lives a tiny elongated variety *(Bollingeri)* which is undoubtedly descended from *subula*. Given this present pattern of distribution, and what is known of the subfossil forms of the lacustrine chalk, it seems almost certain that the formation of the shortened shell phenotypes has preceded that of varieties 4 and 5 *(lacustris* and *bodamica).*

Having said that, however, genotypes 4 and 5 must still be characterized as regards their morphological features and their exclusively lacustrine development. We can then be more certain that they are, in fact, a product of the lengthening of shortened phenotypes. This is not, however, to form any prior conclusions concerning the nature of this lengthening or the mechanism responsible for it. The shortening of the shell in *Limnaea* can be expressed in terms of the relationship between the greatest height of the shell aperture and the overall height of the shell. An average value for this relationship is obtained by the measurement of large numbers of specimens from the populations of selected sites: the resulting figure may be termed the index of contraction. Among those sites inhabited by still water varieties, this index is found to range between 1.65 *(turgida)* and 1.89 *(subula).* Sixty-five thousand individuals were examined (specimens derived from the whole of French Switzerland, part of German Switzerland and Ticino, and from the considerable collections housed in many European museums): the index of the first millesimal (the dividing line between the shortest individual and the remaining 999 of a thousand) averaged 1.529 (reduced to 1.53).[1] Populations of varieties *lacustris* and *bodamica* (which has the same shortened form but is strengthened by a thick marginal rib around the upper side of the aperture) gave averages ranging from 1.31 to about 1.45: the shortest individual index was 1.14, and the general average for varieties 4 and 5 living in lakes was 1.35. It should be added here that *Limnaea stagnalis* is of course very common, and has been described in a great many studies of animal life published since the beginning of the nineteenth century: yet these shortened forms have never been reported as occurring outside the larger lakes of countries within their range. To establish that these varieties *lacustris* and *bodamica* were in fact hereditary, a method was adopted which involved rearing many specimens in the aquarium. They were reared in identical glass bowls, of one-liter capacity, and on an identical diet of salad leaves. It was found

---

1. This average was found to be very constant, after about thirty to forty thousand measurements.

that precise distinctions could be made between varieties 1-5 over five or six successive generations of each variety, with each representing animals gathered from a number of different natural locations. The averages recorded were as follows:

1	2	3	4	5
(subula)	(species type)	*(turgida)*	*(lacustris)*	*(bodamica)*
1.85	1.78	1.68	1.54	1.43

This showed clearly that we were dealing with very distinct and stable genotypes (or genetic pools). Moreover, crossing between varieties 1 and 5 led to a Mendelian segregation at the second generation of descendants.

(I B) All the foregoing evidence would certainly suggest that the hereditary varieties developed as successors to shortened phenotypes. There remains to be answered, however, a significant objection to this conclusion, put forward by E. Guyénot. His point was that these shortened forms might arise from entirely random mutations — in other words, that they could develop anywhere, in marshes as well as in lakes, but would then be eliminated from stagnant waters by some kind of selective factor (a lack of sufficient oxygen, for example). In 1927, to test this, a number of egg-sacs of variety 5 were placed in a pond on the Vaudois Plateau which had never contained *Limnaea stagnalis*. The specimens which emerged from these eggs completely preserved their shortened lacustrine form. Though the pond unfortunately dried up in 1943, the 927 individuals taken from it before that date showed an average index of contraction of 1.39 (which is halfway between the average of 1.35 shown in lakes and that of 1.43 in the aquarium). It is therefore quite evident that variety 5, at least, is well able to survive in stagnant water while preserving its original characteristics. From this we can infer that we are not dealing merely with a random mutation which might occur anywhere. If development of this genotype is linked to limiting and exclusive lacustrine conditions (in which varieties 2 and 3 already develop shortened phenotypes), there must be some relationship between this phenotype and the corresponding genotype. In fact, the latter succeeds the former and constitutes its phenocopy; but the process by which this development occurs remains wholly to be clarified.

(II A) In the course of studying the fall of secondary branches in *Sedum*, we made the chance discovery (already mentioned) of a very small variety of *S. sediforme* not previously described. This variety, which we called *parvulum*, turned out to be hereditary. This kind of systematic variation is also found in several other species of *Sedum*. The *Sedum album* has the well-known variant *micranthum;* the *S. ternatum* (native to the U.S.A.) and *S. anglicum* have the smaller forms which

Praeger named *minus*. This latter dwarf variety is widespread among the rocks of the Bronx botanical gardens in New York. We have transplanted several clumps to Geneva, where they have maintained their diminutive size, growing alongside the normal *anglicum*. The *S. Ewersii*, similarly, has a smaller variety *homophyllum;* and the *S. hispanicum* a variety *minus* or *glaucum* of the same kind. Close study of the new variety *parvulum* is of interest, therefore, in the context of the high degree of variability shown by *Sedum sediforme*. Such study should center on the problem of the phenocopy, since in some situations phenotypes closely resembling *parvulum* can be found. Some preliminary details are necessary, however, to place the problem in proper context.

The *S. sediforme* Jac. (known also as *Nicaense* All. or *altissimum* Poiret) is the largest European species of the group *reflexum,* and is very widespread around the Mediterranean. Its size is difficult to state in general terms because of its polymorphism, but our concern is with the measurement of its leaves, which are fleshy and mucronate. In the case of the "type" of the species, which we will call *altissimum,* the average length of these leaves (from the axil to the base of the

FIGURE 4
Branch of *Sedum altissimum* (life-size).

mucro or terminal point) is about 14 mm (fig. 4), whereas in *parvulum* the average is only 6-6.5 mm (fig. 5). Naturally there are intermediate forms between these two, centering around a quite stable form which we will call *medium*. This has blue-green leaves averaging 9.5-10 mm in length (all averages represent hundreds

FIGURE 5
Branch of *Sedum parvulum* (twice life-size).

of individual measurements). As for the width of the leaves, this can be best expressed as a percentage of the length, giving a value R for the relationship. For
altissimum, $R = 29$ or thereabouts, for *medium* about 30, and for *parvulum* 38.
The thickness of the leaves is an even more distinctive feature, and can also be
expressed as a percentage of their lengths, giving a value R'. For *altissimum*, $R' =$
about 16, for *medium* 19-20, and for *parvulum* about 27. Several other features of
this latter dwarf variety are distinctive and significant. Its color is almost always a
dark green, rather than blue-green. It also shows a high relative incidence of individuals with deciduous leaves (up to 90 out of 100 plants in moderately well-lit
beds). Above all, an astonishing number of plants develop from the separation and
fall of secondary branches by vegetative reproduction. This vegetative tendency is
already very pronounced in *altissimum* and *medium,* but not to the same degree.
These peculiarities of the variety *parvulum* would seem to be characteristic of an
adaptation to difficult conditions or situations —quite different, certainly, from the
southerly locations in which *S. sediforme* usually flourishes. As has already been
noted, the small overall size (involving an increase of surface area in proportion to
volume)[2] improves the efficiency of processes of alimentation. The short but thick
leaves are full of fluid reserves, and the green color is evidence (as Professor
Grépin's measurements show) of more abundant chlorophyll and greater photosynthetic powers than are possessed by blue-green leaves. To these features are
added the possibility that the leaves may be shed in the absence of full sunlight,
and the remarkable capacity for asexual reproduction (with a relative lack of
flowers).

---

2. To objectify (despite the difficulty of measurement), the general height of the stems in *altissimum*
is up to 20 or 30 cm; whereas those of *parvulum* rarely exceed 10 cm. Whole beds of the latter only
contain plants 2-4 cm high.

This variety *parvulum* occurs in great numbers, for instance, along the many gravelled paths of the largest cemetery in Geneva as well on the stone work of a grave too long neglected to provide any hint of the plant's origin. Most interestingly, the plant's near-spontaneous propagation continued despite attempts to clear it before weed-killers were used.[3] Specimens were transplanted to our garden in Geneva and grown under varying conditions. Others were transplanted to rock gardens (also near Geneva, owned by a colleague, A. Rey), to plots in Valais (at altitudes of 900 and 1600 m), and to rocky locations at these same altitudes. In all these situations, the *parvulum* form proved remarkably constant, reproducing itself principally by vegetative means but also sometimes sexually. Believing that this variety represented an adaptation to situations beyond those normally encountered by the species, we therefore investigated its reaction to conditions marginal to its distribution, both in terms of altitude and northerliness. We were fortunate to find examples on la Bérarde (at about 1700 m), but these were blue-green in color (perhaps the effect of solar radiation at altitude): when grown in lowland habitats they preserved this characteristic. Small green forms were collected at several sites near Valence and around Bagnères-de-Luchon in the Pyrenees, and also at an altitude of about 1000 m not far from Barcelona. Green *medium* forms were found at Tibidabe as well. The small green forms were interesting in that they were intermediate between *medium* and *parvulum,* but some phenotypes among them showed all the characteristics of *parvulum.* The same forms were observed at la Drôme and on Mont Ventoux, but here their color was blue-green. We did find, however, among the thousands of specimens grown in Valais and at Geneva, some green plants which reverted to the *medium* form, but this was exceptional. Such plants had previously constituted phenotypes of *parvulum* appearance, rather than genotypes of the variety.

The following conclusions seem reasonable: the *S. sediforme-parvulum* itself constitutes a local genotype, having succeeded phenotypes with the same apparent characteristics. This is similar to the case of the dwarf, high altitude variety of *Sedum album,* i.e., *micranthum.* Unlike the less common genotypic *micranthum* however, *parvulum* attains the status of a local genotype by virtue of very widespread phenotypes. As in the case of *Limnaea,* though, there remains the problem of how we are to understand the mechanism of this succession or replacement. These two very different examples share the common factor of adaptations to somewhat abnormal circumstances. The *Limnaea* faces the necessity of adapting to a dangerously turbulent environment; the *Sedum* must adapt to climatic conditions to which the species is unaccustomed. In both cases, phenotypic variation is the result — not of hostility (so to speak) on the part of a threatening environment,

---

3. When these were used, the variety still did not disappear completely. Several clumps with the same characteristic were found about ten years later.

but of the organism tending to extend its environment and add to its own capabilities. The ultimate genotype, in both cases, attains an equilibrium which the preceding phenotype only sought but did not reach.

(II B) The reader may feel that examples have been dwelt upon which were at once too detailed and too limited. Thorough knowledge of a few cases would, however, seem more useful than easy speculation based upon facts known only secondhand. Given these facts so elementary and so complex, perhaps some extrapolations will be pardoned.

For example, the classic and spectacular cases of hereditary callosity in the warthog, ostrich, and so on, are widely known. These serve a precise function in avoiding injuries caused by contact between the epidermis and the ground. The adaptation culminates, moreover, in a hereditary structural modification, and one which is programmed to occur very early in the course of ontogenic development. On the other hand, the calluses of manual workers, or hardening of the soles of those who walk barefoot, etc., fulfil the same functions but remain largely phenotypic. The difficulty which inevitably faces the observing naturalist is that of imagining what he could have gathered from complex evidence concerning the formation of these tissue modifications had he been present at the time. To suggest that the lucky chance of a random mutation has resolved everything at one blow is to fly in the face of probability calculations which alone can render such verbal solutions acceptable (or rather, quite unacceptable). This is the same as invoking selection without detailing the necessary controls; it takes us no further than the level of fable, or of too facile abstraction. Until there is proof to the contrary, therefore, my inclination is to see these phenomena as resulting from phenocopies. The evidence, of course, is lost, since the events from which such phenomena arose took place long ago.

The same might be said of many other questions. Why, for instance, did mosquitoes begin to bite large animals? How did parasites come to take up residence inside much more highly developed organisms, when in fact their evolution came long before that of their hosts? Unless we postulate a period of phenotypic "trials" which preceded the establishment of the genotypes concerned, are any of these (or similar) phenomena explicable?

One phenomenon is particularly instructive concerning relations between the phenocopy and evolution. Paedogenesis allows an evolutionary line of descent to proceed from the larval stage of ancestral organisms, although the adult form represents a regression from the capabilities of the larva (for example in some sessile echinoderms, whose pelagic larvae possess greater resources). This shows first of all that juvenile initiatives may be richer than those of static or regressive later stages (a fact which might help to explain why the child so often seems more creative and intelligent than the average adult; the regression, alas, being sometimes already apparent in student years). These early trials are not yet lasting phenotypic reactions, but rather the temporary manifestations of capabilities later sacrificed. Second, paedogenesis shows us that the potentials evident in such trials can give rise to formation of higher level genotypes in which the "aspirations" so apparent in the larva but lost in the new genotype's predecessors are restored. Nothing could better express the duality of the opposing tendencies at work here: one conservative and reactionary, the other encouraging an active flexibility. It is this duality which we have noted on several occasions earlier in this study. The third lesson to be drawn from paedogenesis is also the most fundamental. It effectively shows us that the mainspring of new adaptive variations is to be sought primarily in the responses made by epigenetic development to environmental stimuli. This "mainspring" is not to be found right off in mutant modifications of the genome. To note such a lesson is to come to the central idea behind this study: that evolutionary innovations are due not to direct environmental influences, but to the organism's active variation in relation to its environment, and thus to action exerted *on* rather than *by* this environment. Actions of this kind will be the more numerous and effective in that they arise within the hierarchical system of epigenetic development.

To sum up: the examples we have used *(Limnaea lacustris* and *Sedum parvulum),* although quite simple and unpretentious, do at least show that even in such small scale and readily observable phenomena the whole drama of the creation and expansion of life is played out in miniature. By observation with the naked eye, without too great a resort to theory, one can see the extent of the difficulties which arise. In this sense the problem of the phenocopy appears to be that of vital learning in general. It begins with very minor trials, which have no claim to hereditary stability and consequently no guarantee of success, but it ends, however restricted its progress may be, in the creation of stable and transmissible forms. Moreover, the more one comes to accept that evolutionary variations are bound up with innovatory patterns of behavior (a subject to which we will return in the conclusion of this study), the more incontestable becomes the significance of the phenocopy. This is because it is at the relatively free and flexible level of phenotypic explorations that patterns of behavior unforeseen in the hereditary program will have their origins. If the instinctive behavior of animals, which is of course programmed, cannot be so simply explained (and to this too we will return in the conclusion), the whole range of instinctive behavior, beginning with tropisms and the simplest of reflexes, does at least show that modification of organs takes place in constant correlation with behavioral modification. The *Limnaea,* the shell of which is modified by the creature's gripping its stone, serves as a little example of this (ascribable to what Cope called a "kinetogenesis"). In plant life, the absence of a nervous system in no way precludes the possibility of there being processes of reaction. *Sedum*, for instance, loses its secondary branches for purposes of vegetative reproduction (the culmination, as we have shown elsewhere,[4] of a long process of morphogenetic preparation). It adjusts its size to prevailing circumstances by a kind of organic calculation of the ratio of volume to surface area; and is capable of enhancing its powers of photosynthesis, etc. All these are processes of reaction: they begin as phenotypic developments — and are thus analogous to behavioral patterns — but subsequently make way for genotypic replacements. In all these cases, the source of evolutionary innovation, as was said concerning paedogenesis, is to be sought not in direct environmental influence upon the organism, but rather in the action of the organism upon its environment. How can one not be struck by the convergence between this apparently general biological law and the work of forms of intelligence, even superior ones? The innovative constructions of intelligence are based on information derived not from objects as such, but from the actions, or even the coordination of actions which the subject exercises upon objects — which, as will again be emphasized in part II of this study, is not all the same thing. In the fields of cognitive development, the elaboration of such operatory structures (founded, that is, upon the internalized actions which constitute operations) are themselves preceded by tentative empirical trials. These would seem to correspond to initial phenotypic reactions, just as the eventual operatory structure would seem to correspond to the genotypic structure. Here, too, one finds the equivalent of a kind of phenocopy: the final structures replace, and meanwhile partially imitate, behavioral patterns initially dominated by the pressure of what is given. If, as this study proposes, the phenocopy is conceived as an imitation of the phenotype by the genotype, and not the reverse, the problem of understanding the mechanism by which this replacement becomes possible will then be even more acute.

---

4. J. Piaget, Observations sur le mode d'insertion et la chute des rameaux secondaires chez les Sedum, *Candollea* 21-22 (1966): 137-239.

4. Examination
of the Known Hypotheses

The phenocopy is capable of three kinds of interpretation. The first would deny that there is any relationship other than the purely fortuitous, between the phenotype and the corresponding genotype. In other words, the notion of the phenocopy is illusory, and is based upon mere coincidence. The second kind of interpretation suggests that the phenotype does imitate or copy the genotype. Here, however, two resulting possibilities must again be distinguished, depending on whether the phenotype's formation is taken as preceding that of the genotype, or the reverse. Third, the genotype may be interpreted as imitating a previous phenotype, in which case the terms "imitation" or "copy" will not necessarily signify the usual directly dependent relationship. Once again, two possibilities follow. One interpretation would be to consider the genotype as simply a hereditary fixation of the phenotype which would hark back more or less explicity to the Lamarckian transmission of acquired characteristics. The alternative solution, which will be adopted here, accepts that the so-called copy is in reality a reconstruction based upon organic selection. This involves feedback from the phenotype to the genes which regulate epigenetic development, but feedback which does not provide information as to what must be done. It only indicates the presence of states of disequilibrium. These then trigger off the genetic variations of the scanning procedure, variations which are sorted and directed by organic selection (chapter 5).

(I) The hypothesis denying any relationship between phenotype and genotype has never, to my knowledge, been set out in any published form. It was, however, proposed by E. Guyénot in connection with the present study of the lacustrine *Limnaea*. His justification was that the apparent convergence peculiar to this so-called phenocopy was in fact due merely to the small number of variations possible in the species. Thus it was caused by too narrow a range of acceptable kinds of variation. On the one hand, this argument contains a significant exaggeration. It is in fact conceivable that streamlining mutations might have occurred, or mutations involving thickening of the shell, and so on. The latter do arise in a number of marine species, which although elongated are not threatened by turbulent environments. On the other hand (and above all), this hypothesis is open to another objection. If we accept that all convergence between a phenotype and the corresponding genotype is due to a limitation of possible variations, we are led to dispute the purely random character of mutations. We would then accept, as does L. L. Whyte, that mutations are themselves subject to regulation arising from such limitation; subject, for example, to the firmly integrated internal environment of the germ cells. We would be led, in other words, towards acceptance of a process of organic selection. There is, moreover, nothing to oppose the internal environment being directly influenced by the external one. Such influence would certainly not produce an internalized environmental replica, but could occur through the play of the possible disequilibriums of exogenous origin. This is because in situations likely to call a phenotype into being, the external environment imposes a framework of conditions promoting deviation, conditions which could hardly be disregarded.

Briefly then, the denial of a direct relationship between phenotype and genotype in considering the phenocopy leads necessarily to the implicit assumption that indirect relationships exist. It is this implication that we seek to make explicit.

(II A) The usual interpretation of the phenocopy is that the phenotype copies, in advance, a genotype which has yet to appear. Hovasse evades this difficulty by imagining that the phenotype in question would possess a "realizing mechanism, a variant of a genetic or perhaps of a plasmogenic mechanism." Such a mechanism would moreover, according to Hovasse, feature in all phenotypic variations: "The fact that an organism can react to environmental influences implies that, in its cytoplasm, independent of its genes, such a realizing mechanism may exist." These initial suppositions will of course require close examination; but we would first note their corollary, concerning the subsequent formation of the genotype which has thus been copied beforehand: "Once this mechanism has been put into effect, will it not be triggered off again more readily, at a later stage, by a genetic phenomenon? The exogenous somatic modification would then instigate, as it were, the mutation." This would explain the frequency of those situations where a phenotype is "replaced" by a genotype: situations "which then seem somehow to imitate the transmission of acquired characteristics."[1] Hovasse gives the example of *Solana dulcamera* (variety *marina*, with thick, hairy leaves), and distinguishes

1. [mécanisme réalisateur, déviation d'un mécanisme génique ou peut-être plasmogénétique... Le fait qu'un organisme peut réagir à une action du milieu, implique, dans son cytoplasme, indépendamment de ses gènes, la possibilité d'un tel mécanisme réalisateur... Ce mécanisme, une fois réalisé ne peut-il être déclenché à nouveau plus facilement ensuite par un phénomène génique? La somation amorcerait en quelque sorte la mutation.] All quotation is from the *Biologie* volume of the *Encyclopédie de la Pléiade*, p. 1679 — Trans.

three phases in its development. First comes a nonhereditary adaptation. This is followed by a combination of exogenous modifications and mutations which parallel the phenotypic adaptation because they are selected in the same way. Finally there is "complete replacement of the phenotypic adaptation" by the variety *marina* which has become genotypic. It is evident how closely these phases parallel those which this study has just indicated for *Sedum sediforme* (variety *parvulum*). The complexity of the first part of this interpretation shows clearly enough how difficulties will arise for those wishing to support the idea that a phenocopy involves convergence between the initial phenotypic variation and the final genotype without the latter being derived from the former or the phenotypic form being already determined by hereditary variation. It is this problem which has led to the ingenious compromise of the "realizing mechanism." Although endogenous, this would still be capable of "reacting to environmental influences." It would also remain close enough to the genome (insofar as it represents a deviant form of genetic or plasmogenic mechanism) to be able subsequently to trigger off or instigate the mutation which would resemble the exogenous modification.

But what is, in the end, a realizing mechanism, and why should it be deviant from a genetic mechanism? If we accept (recalling chapter 1) the succession through hierarchical levels of the genomically controlled syntheses directing epigenesis, the production of a new phenotypic variation certainly involves the intervention of genetic mechanisms. These aim, however, not to seek out modifications, but only to respect the hereditary program as far as possible while submitting, despite themselves, to variations imposed by the environment. The phenotypic adaptation will thus be the product of equilibrium between these two opposing forces. Only if we overlook this antagonism can we consider Hovasse's realizing mechanism as if it were one of the necessary stages of epigenetic development. If it were seen as such, this realizing or potentiating quality would result from a greater relative flexibility, and would thus be more likely the higher the level of development concerned. What is difficult to understand, though, is the necessity for a particular supplementary mechanism, understood as deviant from the general mechanisms involved. Every genotype is, after all, always embodied in phenotypes, and any epigenetic process always implies interactions between the environment and synthetic processes. When there is change in the environment, certainly new phenotypic variations will arise, but here the modification will still be due to the environment. The role of the endogenous developmental syntheses, on the other hand, is to conserve as far as possible the hereditary program, while at the same time showing evidence of a flexibility consistent with the relevant norms of reaction. For example, in the case of *Limnaea* shown in figure 3 (chapter 1), the way in which morphogenetic synthesis functions can be seen clearly enough. At one time it follows fully its hereditary program (lower half of the shell); at another, it must compromise with a deviation imposed by water turbulence (upper half). If the first section of this shell had been constructed according to a special realizing mechanism, it is very difficult to understand what happened to it while the second (lower) section was being constructed. This lower half is, of course, itself constructed in interaction with the environment, since the species type (or variety 2 genotype) is also embodied in phenotypes which are widely dominant in statistical terms. In view of this, we might well suppose that the construction of this second half of the shell would require a second realizing mechanism. This would amount to the suggestion that such mechanisms must be as numerous as are the diverse forms for which they are supposedly responsible, which is the same as saying that they are inextricably mingled or confused with the general processes of epigenetic development which are in constant interaction with the environment.

Having said that, however, a complete mystery remains concerning the second part of Hovasse's explanation. Even if production of the new modification is attributed to a new realizing mechanism (itself a matter of a differentiation of very general synthetic processes), how can it subsequently trigger off, or simply instigate a mutation resembling the phenotypic variation? This point is central to the whole problem, and the alternatives which it leaves us are neither of them very satisfactory. On one hand, the modification's realizing mechanism might already potentially contain the new mutation. This possibility is fraught with implications, however, since the mechanism is subject to environmental influence. We might just as well affirm, therefore, that the environment acts upon the genome itself; which would be to revert to the Lamarckian interpretation which Hovasse evidently rejects. On the other hand, if this is not the case, we are left to explain how an exogenous modification's realizing mechanism can subsequently be the source of a mutation — of a mutation, moreover, which culminates in the same morphological result. In other words, the mystery remains complete. How is it that a variation arising at the higher levels of epigenesis, under inevitable environmental influence, can prove capable of regaining the lower levels and of finally affecting the genome itself? Such questions as this explain why Mayr, with a great many others, considers that the production of the phenocopy still remains "genetically obscure."[2]

The underlying idea involved here, however, may be that once the exogenous modification has developed, it will, along with its internal environment, constitute a kind of limiting framework.[3] Subsequently, mutations arising in the usual man-

---

2. E. Mayr in Anne Roe and G. G. Simpson, *Behavior and Evolution* (New Haven: Yale University Press, 1958), pp. 354-5.

3. J. P. Faure (*Bull. Biol.* 1973, p. 24) speaks here of an "adaptation-valve," for what we could call a "framework" or "matrix." (See p. 335 of *Biologie et Connaissance*, 1967).

ner will find themselves subjected to a process of selection; not only in terms of the external environment, but also in terms of its internal counterpart (which would explain the instigation). This would imply, then, the intervention of an organic selection in accordance with the Baldwin effect,[4] which Hovasse defines simply as the "possibility of a phenotypic adaptation's replacement by a mutation."[5] To this process, however, would be added the internal selection referred to, and, moreover, a role assigned to exploration activities. It should be noted that these various features are in fact brought together in the process of genetic assimilation described by Waddington, who himself relates them elsewhere to the Baldwin effect.[6]

(II B) The operation of organic selection can be readily understood in relation to the hierarchy of levels existing in the successive developments of epigenesis. At each stage of these developments, products of the preceding (lower) stage may be subject to selection in terms of modifications produced subsequently, at the ensuing (higher) stage. One example is in itself of fundamental importance. It has been shown that the information proceeding from the DNA is not necessarily transmitted in its entirety to the initial RNA: even at this level the process of sorting may have begun.[7] If this is generally the case, the same will be true *a fortiori* for the passage from this RNA to the ribosome, and from there to other RNA. The extremely complex internal processes of the germ cell, which are varied in their nature and their degree of integration, are thus capable of very relevant effects: they may effectively allow, prevent, or modify the transmission of mutations arising within the DNA. The passage from intracellular mechanisms to intercellular connections, again, will be subject to the possibility of selection imposed by these connections. And the same possibilities of selection will be all the more applicable at the level of the tissues and organs.

Given that the external environment often imposes a degree of modification at the higher levels of development, it may follow, as F. Chodat privately points out, that the internal environment will prove even more variable during the course of development: "reciprocal internal constraints — ranging from interference by genetic information within the cytoplasm to the correlation of organs within the entire being — will, by their variety and the amplitude of their deviations exert a

---

4. See J. M. Baldwin, A new factor in evolution, *American Naturalist* 30, (1896): 441-451 and 536-553).

5. Hovasse, *loc. cit.* p. 1656.

6. *The Strategy of the Genes*, p. 164.

7. Britten and Davidson go so far as to see the selection of redundant "messages" from the DNA as a possible source of new mutations.

morphogenic influence far beyond that of the relatively constant encompassing environment. The differing processes of epigenesis therefore produce a result which merits consideration as an 'endoadaptation.'"[8] If the internal environment already varies in this way by itself, then the possibilities of organic selection will be multiplied. They will, moreover, tend to be directed downwards, towards the lower levels, when the external environment has modified whatever it may at the higher levels of synthesis. But in that case it follows necessarily that the interplay and the effect of such multiple selections can attain stability at any given level without descending further. Furthermore, even if the initial RNA is capable of obstructing the passage of instructions from the DNA, that still does not mean that it modifies this DNA in any way. That in itself is quite another problem, since a selective process will not, as a rule, produce variations, but will rather act as a brake upon them.

(II C) The Baldwin effect is, however, sometimes interpreted as more than a simple process of organic selection; it is seen rather as including exploratory mechanisms.[9] At first sight, such an interpretation seems to contradict a basic fact: that a selective barrier is in itself only a source of choice, not of transformations. This remains true, but there are several ways of imagining selection and as many ways of interpreting variations. There may be, despite appearances, a kind of logic in linking the idea of organic selection with that of exploration.

Contemporary biology has effectively distanced itself from the simplistic ideas associated with orthodox neo-Darwinism. The model of selection envisaged by these ideas was merely a process of sifting, by which individuals best capable of survival were retained and others eliminated. On the one hand, selection has appeared increasingly complex: many stages are involved, relating to variables which are no longer measured on an all-or-nothing basis, but as a wide variety of coefficients (of survival, but also of reproduction, recombination, etc.). On the other hand, and most importantly, selection has ceased to be envisaged as an automatic sorting process: it is seen more and more as bound up with processes of regulation and even of choice, in that the organism is capable of choosing its environment before suffering or confronting its constraints. Organic selection is thus bound up with devices or regulators, each showing a certain flexibility and, above all, a cybernetic teleonomy. As such, it is certainly much closer to a system of choice than is selection imposed by the external environment.

This being so, logical symmetry demands a refinement of the concept of

---

8. F. Chodat, quoted in a footnote to the present writer's aforementioned article on *Sedum*, pp. 221-222.

9. Baldwin introduces this interpretation himself.

variations. While selection was conceived as an automatic sifting or filtering, and its results measured only by their success or failure, the corresponding notion was naturally of chance variations, and in particular of purely random mutations. One result of the cybernetic revolution in biology has been to bring selection closer to the idea of choice, or even to the correction of errors by teleonomic feedbacks. Variations, correspondingly, have come to be considered as explorations or trials, according to the model of groping by trial and error. This question has already been touched upon as concerning the production of phenotypic variations (chapter 2). In many cases these adaptations appear less as the result of a one-way determinism than as manifestations of a tendency to exploit all the possibilities of a more or less variable environment or flexible norm of reaction. At the various levels of epigenetic development, therefore, and of organic selection itself, it is all the more likely that selection will apply not to simply passive variations, but to variations which include a certain margin of exploration.

If, however, such explorations occur at every level where some interaction with the environment must be taken into account, what of the purely endogenous production of mutations? Following mathematical study and consideration of the germ cell's integration, Lancelot L. Whyte (and subsequently Britten and Davidson) developed the hypothesis that such mutations are in fact subject to a kind of regulation. They are conceived as deploying themselves over a limited field; and this in itself reduces the purely random element in their development. If we accept this, then the reciprocal question inevitably arises: will not these mutations, within the limited field thus assigned to them, constitute a kind of scanning which amounts to exploiting all its possibilities?

It seems, in conclusion, that if we accept that a relationship between a phenotype and the corresponding genotype is fundamental to the phenocopy, and that the first precedes the second, then we cannot say that the phenotype copies the as yet unrealized genotype. The whole problem of the replacement of an exogenous somatic modification by a mutation therefore remains. The phenotypic variation may, however, arise within a framework imposed by the environment which in turn brings about some modification of the internal environment. Insofar as we accept this, the concepts of organic selection and explorations selected by it will help us to explain how a purely endogenous variation (which we ascribe to the genome) will come to be inserted into the framework imposed at the outset. Such a mutation will develop within a preestablished framework which imposes its own selection as to the adequacy of variations. However exploratory — if not random — we take these mutations with a preestablished framework to be, we have still to understand why it is that mutations are produced in the first place: the organism could, after all, have been left in an apparently stable state of phenotypic adaptation.

A second possibility remains to be considered: that the phenotype in fact copies a genotype formed already, before the occurrence of any analogous somatic modification. This has at at least the virtue of preserving the logical and customary sense of the term "copy." Under natural conditions, however, one can never be sure that a genotype has not been preceded somewhere by a corresponding phenotype. This is certainly the case with environmental adaptations properly so called (as opposed to such features as the color-banding of the *Cepea nemoralis*). Even if this were not the case, on the other hand, then the hypothesis that mutations are adapted from the start to an observable environmental feature (turbulent water, etc.) would still face the same difficulties as before, but in more acute form.

(III A) Finally, we must examine the third possible interpretation: that there is a relationship between phenotype and genotype, but that the latter copies the former and not, as is usually believed, the reverse. This is in fact the interpretation which will be adopted here, and will be developed in a particular form in chapter 5. We should first, however, pause to examine previous accounts, whether known or conceivable, which employ this kind of interpretation.

The simplest, naturally, would be the Lamarckian version: the exogenous modification would constitute an acquired characteristic, and sooner or later it would become capable of hereditary transmission. Only two years ago very few writers would have held to such an opinion. Since then, however, spectacular and unforeseen events have occurred — so much so that Pierre-Paul Grassé, who has never been noted for naïveté, could write an article in November 1972 entitled *The Inheritance of Acquired Characteristics: Still an Open Question.* [10] The reason for renewed belief in this possibility was the discovery by H. W. Temin and Saloshi-Mizudani of a type of enzyme in the RNA of the virus causing chicken sarcoma. This enzyme, "reverse transcriptase," transfers its genetic information into the DNA of the infected cell. D. Baltimore, Spiegelman, and others then found that the same process was at work in various other known carcinogenic viruses. Summarizing these discoveries in a review article, G. Chedd announced them under the title *RNA to DNA: A Revolution in Reverse.*

In cases such as these, the action of the viral RNA on the DNA of the host cell consists in the introduction of the former's carcinogenic property. In view of this, some might wonder whether a kind of parasitism is not involved, and whether the hereditary sequel of the transference by "reverse transcriptase" would not be comparable to some kind of poisoning of the germ. But Beljansky and his colleagues have added further evidence. By treating cultures of *Bacterium coli*

10. Une question toujours ouverte : l'hérédité des caractères acquis, *Savoir et action*, November 1972, pp. 13-24.

with an antibiotic, they isolated resistant individuals. These contain an RNA of which a fractional quantity introduced into a culture of carcinogenic bacilli will cause them to lose this power, the modification then being hereditarily transmitted. In this case there can no longer be any question of parasitism. The acquired characteristic, though, remains negative, and we may still wonder what would have been the outcome had there been a positive transformation, rather than a suppression, within the DNA.

Coming back to the phenocopy, we can then see that it is no longer quite unthinkable, as it still was recently, to accept direct transmission of the Lamarckian type. This would involve the acquisition of characteristics by the phenotypic adaptation, and the subsequent formation of a genotype by which they would become hereditary. Yet we will not keep to such an interpretation here for two reasons. The first concerns the difference between the Lamarckian model (virtually direct environmental influence over the formation of a mutation adapted to it) and the model by which mutations arise endogenously but are subject to selection by external and internal environments. The difference here, as far as the role of the environment is concerned, is only between a simple causality and a probabilist causality: the final effect is the same. The probabilist causality is, however, more satisfying to the mind if the selection concerned is not reduced to all-or-nothing terms of survival or death. As for the role of the organism, in the Lamarckian model it remains passive, subordinated to every external pressure. In this respect the other model, with its hypothesis of endogenous formation and its selections envisaged more as choices, is quite different, particularly in the matter of organic selection, which is directed by a complex system of regulation at every stage of development. Here one is brought to recognize that there exists in every living being a number of fundamental and integrated activities whose combination with behavioral patterns, and ultimately with intelligence, is better assured.

(III B) The outstanding botanist Robert Chodat often used to say that the great mystery about evolutionary variation arose from the everyday observation of phenotypic adaptations which "fix themselves" at some given moment in the form of stable genotypes, but without the mechanism of this fixation being known in any way. Chodat was no Lamarckian, and thus could not consider this problem resolved or even close to resolution. Instead, he simply established what he believed to constitute this fixing, and emphasized that nothing was known as yet concerning the mechanism behind it. His son Fernand Chodat subsequently put forward the hypothesis that "fixing genes"[11] operate to consolidate the heredity of phenotypic

---

11. "Gènes fixateurs" — Trans.

acquisitions, but this clearly leaves us in need of details as to how such genes are developed and how they function.

In any case, for present purposes we should hesitate to accept this idea of the fixing of the phenotypic adaptation. The available evidence permits us only to record that a resemblance (often, in fact, a complete isomorphism) exists between the phenotypic adaptation and the genotype which subsequently comes to replace it. Such a replacement is open to two quite distinct interpretations. It might occur as a consequence of the fixing referred to — this is clearly conceivable. On the other hand, it could represent the reconstruction, or endogenous reconstitution, of a variation which in its phenotypic form was imposed by the environment. Any stable phenotype, of course, will be re-formed under the same environmental conditions in each succeeding generation without hereditary transmission. This may be the case with smallness of size, for example, or the acquisition of any number of habits, not to mention human languages. The striking fact remains, however, that a stable phenotype of this kind does not necessarily give place to a fixed genotype or anything like it. We must explain, therefore, not only how or why an exogenous modification seems in certain cases to trigger the production of corresponding mutations, but also why this happens only under certain conditions and not all the time.

(III C) The explanation which seems the most natural is also the one generally accepted where the genotype is considered to copy a previous phenotype. It is suggested by the two models of genetic and epigenetic homeostasis developed by Lerner (1956), and taken up by Ehrlich and Holm in their well-known book *The Process of Evolution* (McGraw-Hill, 1963). Since every phenotype is founded on a previous genetic basis, it follows that selection may favor phenotypic flexibility or adaptability if variation occurs in the environments of successive generations. On the other hand, where the environment is constant and well differentiated, a standard phenotype will be produced by the canalization of epigenetic processes. The same selective factors will also act upon the canalization of the mutations themselves. Because of this a new genotype imitating the earlier phenotype will be genetically fixed once a certain threshold or plane of selection has been reached. This threshold is set up because the genes become "coadapted" with correlative modifications of several distinct factors. Thus the lowering of selective pressure (once the threshold has been attained) will not produce a reversion, whereas if the threshold is not attained, no genetic fixing will occur.

This effectively explains why it is that a phenocopy is not developed in every case. What this model lacks, however, is recourse to a heuristic dimension of interpretation, necessary because our idea of selection is being refined as well as our conception of the internal organization of the genome. Insofar as the selective factors at work remain external, we can still, of course, quite happily refer to purely random mutations, since these will eventually be canalized into the culminating genetic fixation. Yet if we reestablish the roles of the internal environment and of organic selection, setting them up as indispensable mediators between the external environment and the genome, then to the same extent we multiply the processes of regulation at work. It then becomes much harder to understand why the feedbacks involved in epigenesis do not proceed to sensitize the regulating genes themselves. Not, of course, that the feedbacks would supply information as to what is happening at higher levels, nor, *a fortiori*, indicate what it would be necessary to construct or reconstruct, but they would signal the presence of any obstruction or disequilibrium when it occurs. Any such failures in the system, if sufficiently constant and deep-seated, will inevitably be propagated closer and closer to the genome itself. New variations, arising in response to these purely negative feedbacks, will thus acquire an exploratory status up to the time of reequilibration. Thus the foregoing considerations of the coadaptation of genes and of the selective threshold suggested by their interdependence are completed, in what seems the most natural manner, by this heuristic dimension. This is, in fact, what we must now seek to demonstrate.

5. The Model Proposed

The solution arrived at here is, in fact, quite simple. As factors in the canalization of mutations, it refers only to those selection processes which are either external or, especially, organic within the framework and the inherited internal environment of the phenotypic form. The only factors referred to as causing these mutations are the disequilibriums developed within this internal environment and the resulting attempts to reestablish equilibrium. These points are best explained, however, by using material from chapters 1-3.

I (1) It is clear, first of all, that if the environment imposes new conditions to which a species is not preadapted, or if populations belonging to this species choose such an environment despite its unusual conditions, then a new external framework is created. The features of this new framework, to which the processes of epigenetic development must now be fitted, can be given the symbols x, y, z. Thus a new phenotype will be produced by interaction or compromise between these internal processes (derived from the hereditary or genotypic programming) and the effects of these external features x, y, and z.

(2) This phenotype will then show the characteristics x', y', and z', corresponding to the exogenous factors x, y, z. This correspondence may take any form whatever, as may the manner of the action of x, y or z upon x', y' or z'. In the case of *Limnaea*, for example, x may be the water turbulence and x' the shortening of the shell; here the effect of x upon x' is achieved by way of several mediating effects which include the animal's movements and muscular reactions.

(3) It must then be recalled (from chapter 2) that the actions of x, y, and z upon x', y', or z' may extend to different levels in the hierarchy of stages which is characteristic of epigenesis; thus distinct forms of phenotype will be developed. In the case of *Limnaea*, the external factor x (water turbulence) causes modification at the behavioral level, at the organ level (represented by the shell), and at the level of

the tissues (inasmuch as the shell is secreted by the epidermis). It is doubtful, however, that the phenotypic modification has any further repercussions at lower levels. In the case where multiple enironmental factors (x, y, z) produce diminutive phenotypes of *Sedum* (analogous to the variety *parvulum*), then the small size, green coloration, etc. (x', y', z'), will involve organs and tissues, and no doubt intercellular connections as well. The morphological repercussions of these difficult conditions x, y, and z will undoubtedly be more profound than those arising from the simple mechanical effect which changes the shape of a shell.

(4) In every case it is thus necessary to distinguish two kinds of effect which result from the actions of external factors x, y, and z. In the first place there are the direct or morphological effects, of which the most important will be visible and others will be apparent when examinations are made on an appropriate scale. But possible secondary effects, indirect and essentially functional in nature, must also be considered. These would include disturbances or disequilibriums more or less felt at levels of epigenetic development lower than those where direct effects are still being manifested. This distinction is particularly evident from the fact that the combined processes of epigenesis, directed by the genetic program, constitute a highly integrated system. The internal coherence of this system is ensured by regulation at each level (each comprising a total system in itself), and, most importantly, by further regulation in the hierarchical connections linking lower (earlier) levels with higher levels (their developmental successors). It is therefore necessary to make careful distinction between the two kinds of effects just described. First, the direct or morphological effects (which we therefore call effects x', y', and z') result from the action of factors x, y, and z at one or more specific levels. They are produced by the interaction between these factors x, y, z, and the regulating mechanisms characteristic of these levels. Second, though, there also exist these connections or interregulations between lower and higher levels, conforming to the vertically ascending direction of epigenetic construction. Modifications occurring at the higher levels are thus capable of bringing about disturbances of equilibrium in terms of the vertically descending direction, but these will not be apparent as such, morphologically. Their results, which we will call features x'', y'', or z'', must on no account be forgotten if we are to understand the circumstances in which new genotypes, belonging to the phenocopy, are formed.

(5) It must further be added that, since modifications produced by formation of the phenotype can thus lead to disturbances of equilibrium, attempts to regain equilibrium will naturally be forthcoming in response. These will be more or less successful depending on the viability of the phenotype concerned. It must be

remembered that such gropings or trials occur at every level, and are manifest as various kinds of tentative and exploratory activity.

(6) All in all, although viable, the new phenotype presents the appearance of a complex system whose internal environment is modified in the direction of forms either more or less stable or unstable because it involves certain equilibrated connections but also sources of possible disequilibriums which may be more or less extensive or profound. This complexity results from that of the interactions between processes of epigenetic development and new characteristics imposed by the environment.

II (7) We must now account for the formation of the genotype which will at a given moment replace this already viable phenotype. It might suffice here, as a first approximation, to invoke the production of purely random mutations, but selected as much by the new internal environment as by the external. Among such chance mutations, the external environment (still constituting the same framework, with the same features x, y, z) would accept only those with properties (x', y', z') analogous to those of the preceding exogenous modification. On the other hand, the internal environment (modified as indicated in 4 and 5) would impose its own selective barriers at every level, and random mutations would be sorted just as effectively in passing through them. Ultimately, the genotype emerging from these selective ordeals would be a faithful copy, in every detail, of the initial phenotype.

(8) This solution, however, is only superficially satisfactory, and should not be accepted as it stands. It fails on two very significant counts. In the first place, from the standpoint of survival, this selection of adapted new variations (hereditary, since originating in mutations) serves no real purpose. The preceding phenotype was already viable, and was automatically re-formed with each new generation. To be sure, if any stable phenotype which reconstituted itself in this way (without modification) were to culminate in a phenocopy, then we might imagine that some general economic factor was promoting the replacement of phenotype by genotype. But this is by no means always the case, and thus we have still to explain why such replacement, though it takes place frequently, is not universal. Second (and this probably comes down to the same thing), such an explanation amounts to saying only that the genotype will regain the same general form of equilibrium as was possessed already by the phenotype. The implication, in other words, is of a simple reequilibration, with no concomitant progress or improvement, and thus no sense of any relative optimization. Yet it does seem (as we have sought to illustrate in chapters 1 and 2) that in fact all bioequilibration tends

towards some kind of improvment or enhancement. This is so in the field of organic development (more advantageous variations); it is also evident at the various cognitive levels, from the simplest learned behaviors up to intelligent conduct. Such an improving tendency will develop inevitably sooner or later in proportion to the intervention of teleonomic regulations. This being so, the mechanism by which selections are made should be distinguished in detail, even if (as was supposed in 7 above) the mutations involved remain purely random in origin. Given that modifications of the internal environment in relation to a new phenotypic modification make themselves more or less felt, then mutations will be selected not just for their survival value (hardly meaningful, since the phenotype is already viable), but also in terms of the disequilibriums which complicate and intensify the selective barriers themselves. In other words, the variation most likely to be accepted will be one which reestablishes the threatened equilibrium in the most stable and satisfactory way.

(9) If we accept the strongly integrated character of the regulatory syntheses in the form of loops or cycles at every level, as well as the interconnections between higher and lower levels,[1] then in fact the variation selected can only be the one most liable to comply with a structure. This variation must, that is, be capable of reestablishing the coherence and the closure of these cyclic systems when they are modified or threatened by changes introduced at the time the phenotype is formed. In general, any new mutation, insofar as it modifies the genes, will entail *ipso facto* some degree of alteration of earlier syntheses, and thus a local change in the hereditary program. The consequent problem will be that of reconciling what is new in this synthesis with the properties of those earlier syntheses, rectifying in that way the way the disequilibriums introduced by the new phenotype. In other words, the endogenous variations or mutations which succeed the phenotype must conform to features x, y, and z of the external environment, and to the conditions (partly in equilibrium, partly out of it) of the new internal environment. Insofar as they do conform to these conditions, successful selection will lead to a reestablishment of equilibrium in the synthetic processes themselves. New and former characteristics will then regain a state of mutul dependence befitting a closed cyclic system of regulation (as opposed to the state of simple compromise characteristic of exogenous phenotypic modifications). This indicates both economy and improvement in relation to obligatory accommodations and to the various trials or attempts thwarted by the environment.

---

1. If rightly understood, each of these successive levels of synthesis constitutes what F. Jacob calls an "integron" *(intégron):* a well-integrated system governed entirely by its own laws of totality, and thus possessing its own particular internal regulation. In the same way, an assemblage of "integrons," characterized by what we term its interregulations, would in turn constitute a new "integron."

(10) This kind of interpretation allows us to answer one of the basic questions raised by phenocopies: that of their occurrence being ultimately very frequent, but in no way universal or inevitable. When a phenotype is sufficiently stable and does not threaten to disturb the equilibrium of the epigenetic system, then there is no reason why it should be replaced by a genotype of analogous form. The only progress this would entail would be the substitution of heredity for the phenotype's continual reconstitution in each succeeding generation. On the other hand, if the phenotype is the source of varying degrees of disequilibrium, then the genotype will reestablish a normal interplay of syntheses ensuring precorrection of errors rather than corrections only under constraints.

III (11) In order to account for the new genotype's resemblance to the phenotype which precedes it, we have thus sought to correct the model based upon purely random mutations and selection, particularly by the internal environment. We have also sought to understand how a new mutation (or more precisely, the hereditary fixing of a genetic modification) can culminate in an equilibrium better than that attained by a phenotypic modification. These efforts bring up two questions to be resolved. The first concerns the way the genotypic variation is set in progress or, more precisely, release of the set of such variations, among which the selective functions of the internal environment and epigenetic system will have to choose. The second is the question of the nature of these genetic variations, whether they are now considered only partially, rather than entirely, random in origin.

(12) We may best begin by summarizing in some detail what has so far been concluded concerning those large-scale developments which occur when the course of an organism's epigenesis is modified by the formation of a new phenotype. This process of phenotypic formation will, of course, recur in each succeeding generation for as long as the phenotype itself prevails. The direction of the large-scale developments referred to is of great importance here. The first movement, or vector (symbolized as $\uparrow a$) to be noted is that of normal epigenetic development in accordance with hereditary programming. Movement $\uparrow a$ therefore originates in the DNA of the genome, passes though the RNA into the entire system of the germ cell, with all its different regulations (allosteric or macrocellular), and is then transmitted by way of intercellular connections. It thus reaches the tissues and organs, and ultimately attains the level of behavior, sensitivity, and capacity for reaction. Each of these systems it passes through will have its own laws of totality or autoregulations over and above the fundamental intersystemic controls. A second vector ($\downarrow b$) to be considered — again only in broad terms — runs in the opposite direction, and represents the set of exogenous modifications imposed by

the environment. These are, first of all, the actions intervening at the heart of the direct phenotypic variations x', y', z' which correspond to factors x, y, z in the external environment (chapter 2). These modifications will themselves constitute a selective barrier (not primary but final) capable of influencing the ultimate choice of acceptable endogenous variations. Subsequently, however, the exogenous modifications are the various disequilibriums x'', y'', z'', produced at lower levels than x', y', or z'. Hypothetically, these disequilibriums are themselves also capable of playing a part in the selection (by the internal environment) of endogenous variations being produced in the direction of vector $\mid a$. At this point it must be carefully emphasized that though $\mid a$ vectors transmit forms which are already constructed (since they are inscribed in the information of the DNA), $\mid b$ vectors carry no program whatsoever, and their function resides purely and simply in the indication by feedbacks of obstructions or disequilibriums. This distinction and limitation is implicit throughout this whole interpretation. Consequently, though our $\mid b$ vectors include those exogenous actions which influence the construction of phenotypic characteristics x', y', and z', these actions will not be the only source of these features. In fact, they will have no more direct effect than to set in motion the gropings or exploratory trials which we will call vectors $\mid c$. The other words, the features x', y', and z' are products of the conjunction $(\mid b) \times (\mid c)$, and in no way are products of a preformation programmed by the environment for transmission by vectors $\mid b$. In the case of the disequilibriums x'', y'', and z'', a fortiori, what the feedback $\mid b$ actually transmits will never be a message (comparable to that carried by RNA) conveying "what is happening" or "what must be done." On the contrary, the information transmitted by $\mid b$ vectors will be limited exclusively to the indication that something isn't working. Where $\mid c$ vectors are involved, they will comprise on every level the tentative trials or gropings instigated by conflicts between $\mid a$ and $\mid b$ vectors. These conflicts themselves (the actual result of opposition between the environment and the genetic program) will thus constitute disturbances of equilibrium or deviations from the program, and they will sooner or later be overcome (as when quickly remedied, for instance, by the production of phenotypic variations x', y', or z'). Such conflicts may persist, however, in latent form as sources of real or potential instability. This will be the case when disequilibriums x'', y'', and z'' exist, and when the phenotype is, therefore, entirely stabilized and will consequently become the source of a phenocopy. It should be added that the exploratory trials ($\mid c$), because of their groping nature, can only end at the solutions sought (reequilibrations to eliminate conflicts and disturbances of equilibrium) by means of an interplay of regulations and selection by both external and internal environments, primarily the latter. Organic selection thus contributes in part to a progressive reconciliation among programming ($\mid a$), deviations ($\mid b$), and attempts at their correction ($\mid c$).

IV (13) Two interconnected problems naturally arise from all this. To what level will | b vectors (repercussions or indications of disequilibrium) descend, and from which levels will the signal that something isn't working begin to release responses of type | c?

At higher developmental levels, deviations (|b) and responses (|c) can regularly be observed. In *Sedum* for example, a bud need only be destroyed anywhere on the plant and another will grow beside it. This would never occur unless there were the demand for such a loss to be compensated. Similarly, an undetached branch need only be poorly exposed or a little too dry, and it will put down adventitious roots. Disturbances of equilibrium have thus been signalled (|b), and this signal has reached some level from which a compensatory process of reconstruction can begin. It is clear, though, that such a development (occurring in accordance with epigenetic programming when this has only been opposed at the one point) does not imply retroaction extending back to the origin of the whole system. When, on the other hand, factors are concerned which condition alimentation and life itself throughout the organism's growth (as such factors as size, etc., may do), then inevitably the repercussions of disequilibrium will extend progressively to the most elementary levels.

Our initial hypothesis will therefore be as follows: persistent instances of disequilibrium (x'', y'', z'') arising from the formation of the phenotype will ultimately (thanks to these successive repercussions) sensitize the regulating genes responsible for the fulfilment of the epigenetic program and thus for the syntheses of which growth consists. It must again be emphasized, though, that the signal of such disturbances carried by | b vectors is in no way a differentiated message: there is no precise feedback as to "what is happening" or "what must be done." Thus there is no message nor any messenger, so to speak, distinct from the layers of tissue or cytoplasm the perturbation crosses — there is only the disclosure that a disturbance exists, transmitted as a succession of obstructions which themselves give rise to processes of external selection. Let us say, for example, that A, B, C, D, E are successive levels of syntheses leading from the regulating genes in A to level E. If a disequilibrium (x'') occurs at level E, then normal synthesis will be disturbed or obstructed at that level. Changes will then occur equally at level D, which will in turn disturb the synthetic work at C and thence B. The eventual outcome will be the sensitizing of genetic controls at A.

(14) It should especially be noted that with this hypothetical model we do not have to accept the necessity of a return message from the RNA at B to the DNA at A. The experiments of Temin and Beljansky show that this would seem to be possible in certain cases, through the medium of "reverse transcriptase" (see chapter 4, section III). But we do not know how general this phenomenon may

be, and the present model has no need of it. Here it is enough that the RNA should be slightly modified at level B, or, more precisely, that its operation should be impeded by a relative obstruction at C. It is then no longer as efficient as before in responding to the instigations of the DNA, the result being that this resistance at B has the effect of sensitizing the regulating genes at A. Vector $\mid b$, accordingly, is best thought of along the lines of selective barriers, as a negative signal somehow rather than a positive message. While at higher levels it is the transmitter of observable disturbances, at the levels of origin it can only indicate them as resistances or hindrances to the processes of development. The epigenetic system, as we have noted, is highly integrated: each stage has its own system of regulations, and each is bound to the levels before and after by a complex system of interregulations. If we accept this (and it seems generally established), then it would seem obvious that information in the constructive direction ($\uparrow a$) will imply the existence of return information, as is the case in all cyclic teleonomic systems. Either the processes of development will proceed normally, and there will be no need for specialized signals ("no news is good news"), or disturbances and obstructions will occur. When they do, their existence can be communicated only by retroactive repercussions, by gradually recurrent changes, level by level.

V (15) Our second hypothesis may appear more fraught with implications than the first, yet it is no more than its logical continuation. If, as we have suggested, disequilibriums in the course of epigenesis produce repercussions and these ultimately sensitize the regulating genes, then these genes are sure to respond. Their response will consist of gropings of various kinds, and these may present themselves under two forms. On the one hand, things may simply return to normal without mutations being produced. Simple reequilibration, in other words, may restore the former equilibrium of a genotype already in place. On the other hand, there may appear a whole collection of multiple variations, constituting new mutations among which the internal environment will exercise a selective function. The outcome will be a resemblance between these new mutations and former phenotypic variations, not because there is any "fixing" of phenotypic features, but rather because the conditions of their selection are the same.

Here there is a series of points which will require further comment and justification: (a) the eventual relationship between the production of mutations and epigenetic disequilibriums: in broad terms this might be considered a special case of "paedogenesis" (see chapter 3, section IIB); (b) the semialeatory and semiexploratory nature of these new mutations. In one sense they are formed at random, yet only within the limited field laid open by particular cases of disequilibrium. In a second sense (relating to the borders of this field and to the conditions by which an improved equilibrium might be established) they could be considered to represent assorted trials or explorations; (c) the final resemblance between genotype and phenotype. The genotype is the ultimate product of selection by internal (organic selection) or external environments. Imperfections in the phenotype were responsible for the disequilibriums which occasioned the entire process.

(16) We may begin with the first of these points: connections between the production of new mutations and disequilibriums in epigenetic development. A distinction is often made between abrupt mutations (results of a more or less teratological or even lethal disorganization) which are entirely random, and minor mutations (products of limited fluctuation around a particular genetic characteristic). If this distinction is well founded, it seems naturally to imply some relationship between the two functions of the genome: one of hereditary transmission, the other of instigation and direction of epigenetic development. If minor mutations modify developmental processes, the disturbances of equilibrium which may occur in epigenesis, reciprocally, sensitize their regulating genes and thus modify transmission. This does not, it must be emphasized, mean that acquired phenotypic characteristics are transmitted. There are, simply, repercussions or propagation of disequilibriums in the direction of vector $\downarrow b$ until the genes which direct epigenetic processes are affected. The production of genetic variations or minor mutations will follow, since the genome functions as a complete system — "like an orchestra," in Dobzhansky's words, rather than as a soloist.

It might well be objected, however, that the genes regulating epigenesis are not necessarily the same as those which direct hereditary transmission to subsequent generations and are thus the source of possible mutations. Generally speaking, though, all transmission, including that involving mutations, entails new epigenetic development; but epigenetic processes do not act reciprocally on transmissions by returning positive messages. If this remains true where distinct and superimposed developmental levels are involved, then the answer must be that the genes controlling transmission and epigenesis, even if distinct, must be interconnected. They are, after all, situated at the same level in that both are part of the same genome and contribute to its homeostasis. It must be stressed, moreover, that the reverse signal which (on this hypothesis) sensitizes the genes regulating epigenesis is a negative one, and conveys no positive information: it reports only defects of functioning. It would then be this disturbance which would lead to the production of mutations, through its inevitable connection with the genes responsible for hereditary transmission.

(17) Another preliminary question, however, which could have been raised at (13) and (14) above in the discussion of our first hypothesis, takes on an even greater significance in the present context. Why is it that the signaling of disequilibriums

in the direction ↓b must go clear back to the genome? Given, too, the accepted possibility of exploratory responses and reequilibrations at every level without the need of returning to the point of origin, why should it be up to the genome to react by the production of new variations?

In fact, of course, each cell of an organism contains in its nucleus chromosomes and at least a fraction of DNA. It should therefore be possible, in theory, by virtue of this "total potentiality" of the genetic possibilities of any genotype, for readaptation to occur in any area. Clearly, though, these local systems are subordinated to an overall system: a possible inhibition will of necessity correspond to every positive capacity, otherwise any part of the organism might produce virtually anything. Thus it is obvious that the overall system cannot be reduced to a sum of particular systems or levels. It bears responsibility for the organization of the whole: the coordination of inhibitory factors is as important as that of positive factors, and their interaction as important as their separate functioning. From this it seems possible to conclude that any disequilibrium which involves the entire organism (as in alimentation), and not just this or that part of it, will have an effect extending back to the origins of this overall system. This does not mean, however, that every disequilibrium presents this general character and requires signaling back to the genomic level with release of exploratory variations. Yet this hypothesis would seem necessary in accounting for normal or abnormal situations, or those in which only chronic instability or stable reequilibration are involved.

(18) Our next step must be to justify the conclusion that these new genetic variations will not remain purely contingent, but will be partly exploratory in their nature. An element of chance persists, of course, in any groping or trial; but there is also a kind of scanning of the field of possibilities. We should begin by recalling the supposed mechanisms of organic selection which lead to the choice of acceptable mutant forms over and above selection by the environment.

For present purposes, organic selection is taken to be a sorting or choice among variations. It occurs not only as a function of general features of the internal environment of the genotype embodied in a particular phenotype, but also as a function of the various properties (and degree of resistance or integration) of the regulating mechanisms operating at each level of synthesis during the course of epigenesis. Thus understood, the first achievement of organic selection will be an initial elimination of some variations in favor of others, which will then be submitted to a second process of sorting or choice. This first elimination operates in two ways. One, naturally enough, involves the exclusion of lethal or pathogenic variations; the second, on the contrary, amounts to the hindrance of variations in any direction insofar as these run up against systems which are too stable. This latter directly eliminates variations or brings them back to the right path (what Waddington calls homeorhesis). Thus the variations remaining are those which fall into neither of these categories: in other words, those which affect areas where there is relative but persistent disequilibrium (as may be the case in most new phenotypic situations). In this case, at the time of the second round of eliminations, organic selection is reduced to a kind of equilibration of elementary mechanisms. If a variation will increase the disequilibrium, a selective barrier is automatically erected and it is discarded. If, on the contrary, it will diminish the disequilibrium, then it is accepted. Successive variations will be similarly dealt with. As in any groping process, there may occur fluctuation between partial regression and successive progressions until stability is eventually attained.

(19) At the lower levels of epigenetic development, it seems that the strong integration of the germ cell, in particular, exerts a continual control over mutations. From this arose L. L. Whyte's important conception of a system regulating mutations, which could at one extreme produce "de-mutation" of harmful variations and at the other effect reinforcement of more advantageous ones. Similarly, in 1969, R. J. Britten and E. H. Davidson set out a hypothesis of genetic regulation, the interest of which was in trying to relate innovative mutations to the genetic combinations which precede them. If mutations are themselves subject to regulation, then it does not seem extravagant if we interpret genetic variations which occur as a response to persistent phenotypic disequilibrium (before the phenocopy) as a set of trials or explorations. This does not mean, of course, that there are attempts to copy or fix the positive characteristics x', y', or z' referred to above. It means only that every attempt is made to rectify the disequilibriums x'', y'', and z'', which is not at all the same thing. It may, for example, be a matter of inhibiting an unfavorable characteristic, such as the elongated shell of *Limnaea* living in turbulent lacustrine waters. This was achieved in a stable manner by the genotype *lacustris*. Phenotypes of the same shortened form, on the other hand, were the seat of permanent conflict between their morphogenetic or behavioral characteristics and the characteristics of the hereditary programming of the genotypes of varieties 2 or 3 (see chapter 3). It may, alternatively, be a matter of reinforcing an advantageous characteristic, such as an increase in the chlorophyll content and hence the photosynthetic efficiency of the *parvulum* genotype of *Sedum*. This can only be achieved in the corresponding phenotypes by conflict with the characteristic blue-green coloration which is most usual in the genetic programming of *S. sediforme*. Briefly, then, the few genetic variations arising in such cases as these constitute an exploration of the various possibilities of inhibition and of reinforcement. These possibilities are correlative as the presence of a predicate *a* and the exclusion of those predicates which imply anything other than *a* are in logic. This exploration will continue until a sufficient state of equilibrium is reached.

VI (20) We thus come to the final and decisive problem: that of the resemblance, central to the phenocopy, between the new genotype which copies and the preceding phenotype which is simultaneously copied and replaced. All the foregoing discussion shows clearly enough that, according to our interpretation, there will be neither transmission nor even fixing of phenotypic characteristics, but rather endogenous reconstruction by the genotype. If this reconstruction appears to be a copy after the fact, it is because the genotype has been faced with the same problems as the phenotype — in conflict with the same external environment, and, therefore, within the same framework x, y, z — and because it has resolved these problems by constructing characteristics analogous to the phenotypic x', y', and z', since it was subject to the same selective conditions of the same internal environment as it strove to eliminate disequilibriums x'', y'', and z''. Hence arises the copy of which so much has been said.

The difference between this model and that of Lamarckian transmission is obvious. Let us suppose, as in (13) above, that A, B, C, D, E are the successive levels of epigenetic development. The direct transmission model would then imply that a phenotypic feature x' or y', developed at levels E or D by the interaction between endogenous synthesis and the environment, would by that same fact be introduced into developmental processes at C and B. It would thus, ultimately, modify the genome at A, being registered in the form of a new mutation in the hereditary program of these syntheses. In the model proposed here, on the other hand, the phenotypic characteristics x' or y' will be neither transmitted nor signalled to the regulating genes at A. Instead, because they disturb normal developments at D or E, these alterations or deviations will constitute a sort of blockage or obstacle to be overcome, and it is this that will give rise to the disequilibriums x'' or y'' at levels C and B. It is these disequilibriums and these alone which will sensitize the regulating genes at A, with no information provided as to their cause or nature in E or D, nor, *a fortiori,* as to the morphologic characteristics x' or y'. It is thus, solely by means of feedback to the effect that "something is not proceeding normally" with no indication as to what, that new mutations are produced, since an alteration, however slight, at the level of the genome can only give rise to genetic variations. In this case the variation produced will develop in the direction $A \rightarrow E$ (therefore ↑), whereas in the case of a Lamarckian transmission it would have developed in the sequence $E \rightarrow A$ (therefore ↓).

(21) The problem is therefore to understand why it is that these variations will finally resemble the phenotypic characteristics x', y', or z'. In theory, in the manner of nonoriented gropings, such mutations would be capable of developing in any direction whatsoever. In fact, however, because organic selection (which comes

into operation straightaway) is a function of the internal environment and of all the strongly integrated system of epigenetic syntheses, an initial sorting will be imposed from the very outset, as we have already suggested. Mutations will thus be capable of effective development only in regions of disequilibrium; other regions will remain stable, and therefore resistant.

(22) As for these regions of disequilibrium, the question is as follows. At work, on the one hand, will be the tendencies and forces belonging to the hereditary program of normal epigenetic processes. On the other hand, these will be locally obstructed or deflected, both by constraints of the external environment (x, y, z) and by constraints of the corresponding internal environment responsible for the formation of phenotypic features x', y', and z'. Thus far, these constraints will have exerted a direct causal action, since these phenotypic features x', y', and z' constitute the causal product or effect of their action upon the unfolding of epigenesis. In relation to the genetic variations, on the other hand, such constraints will form nothing more than a restrictive mold or obligatory framework into which the mutations must, as it were, insert themselves. This may be objected to as merely a verbal distinction, on the basis that a mold or framework may itself exert a causal action, or at least a reaction in the sense of Newton's third law (action and reaction). But there is in fact a difference, and it is a fundamental one in that the whole debate between Lamarckism and contemporary biology rests upon such a distinction. Causal constraint exerts a direct action in the sense that its effect will express its positive characteristics. A mold or framework, on the other hand, exerts only a selective action, which is negative in the sense that it will discard variations which do not conform to it and thus impose a process of sorting or choice by means of successive trials. In other words, new genetic variations are produced neither by the external environment nor by its internal counterpart, as phenotypic variations were, but remain totally endogenous. They explore regions of disequilibrium until adequately adjusted to the mold or framework imposed upon them, until this framework accepts them by selection. But the framework does not produce them.

(23) However, since these are endogenous variations, the final solution is very different from that which characterized the initial phenotype, despite the resemblances imposed by a framework which is the same in both cases. In the development of the phenotype, the new external conditions $x, y,$ and z came into conflict with the hereditary epigenetic programming; thus the phenotypic characteristics x', y', and z' constituted only a compromise or an unstable equilibrium between these two kinds of heterogenous influences. In the case of the new genotype, by contrast, it is the epigenetic program itself which is modified

by new mutations once these have been selected by the internal and external environments. Insofar as these mutations can conform with the mold or framework imposed, they will then at the same time be both similar to preceding phenotypes and quite distinct from them: similar through their resemblance (in the characteristics x', y', z'), distinct in that the mutations will be in equilibrium (the opposite of x'', y'', z'') and will henceforth form part of a coherent hereditary program.

(24) The remarkable feature of this new equilibrium is therefore a kind of interdependence between the mutations or variations (in developmental processes and in transmissions) and one or more processes of selection. As far as these selections are concerned, the external mold or framework (x, y, z) is only one of the factors involved. The others, as has already been said, are the developmental processes of epigenesis as a whole and the internal environment: a fundamental part is played, in other words, by organic selection. J. Monod sums this up when he speaks of selection imposed by "the collective structures and operations of the teleonomic system."[2] On occasions when the equilibrium of this system is locally and temporarily disturbed, internal selection will have a double part to play. That one of its roles will be conservative goes without saying, since the general integration of the system must be preserved; but it must also perform a self-correcting role, since mutations must be directed or channelled into regions of disequilibrium. The effect of the variations themselves is similarly a double one: a set of changes on the one hand, but on the other a reequilibration which directs selective pressures while at the same time safeguarding the general outline of the system. Thus if selective processes imposed by the external environment culminate in a local equilibrium between external modifications and the organism, then organic selection, similarly, will achieve equilibrium between the subsystems of a totality, and the result will be a higher level of coherence. In this sense, therefore, the variations invoked will be neither environmentally induced (since they are endogenous) nor strictly aleatory (since they have been channelled by a selective mechanism which they themselves have partially modified or directed). They consist rather in successions of trials or explorations in response to disturbances of equilibrium. We can thus see why, insofar as the idea of selection is oriented in the direction of choice (relative to what Monod calls the "teleonomic system"), the concept of variation can only be considered equivalent to that of directed trials or exploration (scanning). There is, after all, a symmetry in this: channelled genetic variation is directly comparable with what is thought of, on the level of conduct,

---

2. "l'ensemble des structures et performances de l'appareil téléonomique" (*Le hasard et la nécessité*, p. 141).

as groping by trial and error. Both share in the element of chance, but also in a general orientation dictated by the need to reestablish equilibrium.

(25) It is worth emphasizing, finally, that this interpretation of the phenocopy is basically constructivist in nature. The new genotype constitutes the ultimate result of conflicts and interactions between organism and environment, and the environment thus necessarily intervenes as one of the transforming elements in its causality. If this is so (and here lies the constructivism), then the adaptation itself has, as its producing factor, not the environment as such, but rather the constant action of the organism upon the environment, which is by no means the same thing. We have already stressed, at the level of the phenotype, the multiplicity of responses involved. These will tend to range over the field of possibility, each making the best use of prevailing conditions. However, to make use of such conditions is not to submit to them. When a *Sedum,* for instance, has all its stems grow upwards or lets them trail along the ground, and when it brings about the abscission of its secondary branches or retains them only to shed them later, etc., these are surely "strategies," employed as in a game with a partner, and not merely the effects of simple external determination. Even if we discount the factors of light, temperature, soil, and so on, which certainly intervene, they do not act as in a composition of forces; rather they give rise to a kind of assimilation or integration into a teleonomic system dominated by the organism's reactional behavior as a whole. In the case of mutations, the scope of preliminary gropings can be much wider when, in the end, only a single genotype is retained. The same is true, at the level of conduct, when the adjustment of highly complex patterns of behavior is necessary. And from this has arisen the currently widespread notion of purely random productions, subject to selection "after the event." As we have just recalled, however, this final product is, on the one hand, the result of variations which appear as oriented trials or gropings as well as of selective processes, the organic forms of which are equivalent to choices made in terms of the maintenance or improvement of epigenetic regulations. These explorations and choices, yet again, have a teleonomic dimension which attests their active character. On the other hand, selection of the best genotype involves a property which is inherent and fundamental in such self-regulating situations, i.e., the genotype's flexibility: its capacity, in other words, to engender new phenotypes after having replaced one.

These various aspects of the organism's action upon its environment thus seem to confirm the constructive nature of evolutionary variations, even when they are as small in scale as those considered in this study. This seems clear even without returning to the example discussed in chapter 2, which involved an actual extension of the environment. This thesis will, it is true, come up against the predictable objection that all apparent innovation is in fact predetermined in the so-called language of DNA. The "letters" of this language (which in fact is nothing like a language since its information consists of "signifieds" and not "significants"[3]) are established once and for all. All evolution does is combine them in every deducible way, into various "words," "phrases," "chapters," and so on. This is tantamount to the suggestion that, given our alphabet, all books, past and present, are nothing but combinations of letters; but, as G. Cellérier neatly put it, "they still have to be written." In any case, the choice of some combinations would inevitably mean the exclusion of others. Thus there would result a whole collection of historical processes, mutually irreducible, which would multiply relations of order over and above the synchronizable combinations. The notion of any "totality of possibilities" then becomes a paradox because the realization of any one possibility will open up new ones. It is precisely this opening up, according to Rensch, which constitutes evolutionary progress.

---

3. The great linguist Hjelmslev has effectively shown that the existence of any language is linked to that of two systems (the "significants" and the "signifieds"), of which the functional units or their derivations remain heterogenous. It is very different in the case of the genetic code.

Part II

The Cognitive Problems

6. The Cognitive Equivalent
of the Phenocopy

In part II our aim will be to investigate a series of problems relating to intelligence; but we will not be concerned in any detail with the more elementary forms of knowledge, such as perception, memory, habits, and so on. Our main interest in the phenocopy arises, in fact, because the phenomenon seems to play quite a generalized part in the workings of evolution. It provides, most significantly, the beginnings of an explanation of adaptation to the environment, and this cannot fail to interest us if we are dissatisfied with the model which, in relying on random variations and selection "after the event," rests upon an apparently complete improbability. If we suppose that the process of the phenocopy, as interpreted here, is in some degree general, the question naturally follows — if we have any interest in relations between organic life and knowledge — whether there is some equivalent of the phenocopy which is central to cognitive functioning. In this domain, after all, the organism can be said to correspond to the subject, and the environment to the set of external objects that it is a matter of knowing. The problem is in this sense analogous to that of adaptation. The more one makes this hypothesis of a certain generality the higher will be the stages of knowledge and therefore the level of intelligence at which we must attempt to verify our hypothesis.

(I) The comparison we will be outlining may, however, seem paradoxical — or, still worse, meaningless — if we rely upon current ideas which have for long been central tenets of neo-Darwinism in biology and of behaviorism in the study of conduct. The first of these doctrines holds, in effect, that the mechanism of evolution is fundamentally endogenous, and this we would not dispute. But it also holds that the only part played by the environment is an essentially negative one. On one hand, the environment eliminates everything that is not suited to it, which again, of course, we would accept. But on the other hand, it counts for nothing in the case of detailed and differentiated adaptations, like the shape of a fish, the bill of a woodpecker or hummingbird, the callouses of a warthog, and so on. In all such cases (and they are virtually coextensive with the entire range of evolution), the doctrine of neo-Darwinism has only the one answer to offer. On one hand, the capacity of chance alone is considered inexhaustible in the production of any variation whatever, even of such spectacular inventions as these. And on the other hand the role of the environment is once more considered to be purely negative: it is limited to the retention of whatever may be presented to it in the form of preadjusted variations, and this simply because the least advantageous forms are eliminated. It goes without saying that this passive character of the environment and of selection is the great defect of this viewpoint. It is such a considerable omission that even a mind so deeply courageous in its logic as J. Monod's has recently concluded (in a passage already quoted in chapter 1) that evolution is "in no way a property of living creatures" and that it depends only on the "imperfections" in genetic conservation which is perturbed by chance. In short, according to interpretations of this kind, nothing at all is due to the environment, except a capacity for "filtering," and the production of variations is considered entirely endogenous, but with the imperative condition that genetic conservation be enriched through an indefinite submission to the unlimited vagaries of chance.

If we turn to what has long been virtually the official doctrine in the study of behavior, we find precisely the opposite picture. To the extent that the subject (the organism in its behavior) acquires some knowledge, whether the "knowing how" associated with sensory-motor learning or the highest forms of intellection, that knowledge is always attributed to the successful recording of something observable drawn from objects. Thus the external environment constitutes the sole possible source of cognitive progress. In effect, to every external stimulus there will correspond a response in the subject, but defined by Hull in terms of a functional copy of the external situation. In other words, from this second perspective it is the environment which is all-powerful and active, so to speak, in an essentially positive sense, whereas the subject, envisaged purely as a receiver, remains quite passive. Even when Skinner's pigeons depress a lever, this initial action upon the environment leads only to the discovery of more properties of that environment, in order that its variations in the form of positive or negative reinforcement may be endured.

We may be somewhat surprised to see how little attention is given by partisans of each of these "official" doctrines to the assertions made by the other; but logically, of course, there is no contradiction between them. Neo-Darwinism is after all concerned only with genotypic heredity, and behaviorism only with reactions which remain essentially phenotypic, and thus nonhereditary. If partisans on both sides were correct in their beliefs, that would amount to saying that the environment plays a purely negative part at the level of the genotype and an essentially positive one at that of the phenotype. And there would be nothing wrong with that, if there were no relationships between these two levels. Yet if it should be the case, as we have suggested, that the process of the phenocopy presents some generality, then, on the contrary, a serious doubt would be cast upon the validity of these classic hypotheses.

We should therefore indicate from the outset the way in which both these doctrines seem mistaken as regards the role of the environment. In the case of both genotypic variations and of behavior or knowledge, the most important factor should be sought not in the actions of the environment as such — be they negative (mere selection) or positive (the stimulus-response or *SR* schema) — but rather in the actions which the organism or individual exerts *upon* that environment by virtue of essentially endogenous initiatives. In other words, if our interpretation of the phenocopy were to prove at all valid, it would allow us to furnish a common answer to the classic doctrines of both neo-Darwinism and behaviorism. This answer would be that the environment in fact plays a fundamental part at every level, but as something to be ovecome, not as a causal agent of formation. Thus causal agencies would be sought at all levels of endogenous development within the organism and the subject. If it were not for the multiple problems raised by the environment or the outside world, both organism and subject would remain conservatively oriented, and incapable of new invention (like the *Lingula* which have not evolved since the Palaeozoic, or like some human societies — or even some human adults). They can, however, respond to such problems by trials and explorations of all kinds, from the elementary level of mutations to the higher level of scientific theories, but on condition that they do not rely upon chance (deified by so many biologists), and that they are subject to regulations.

From a viewpoint such as this, a degree of generality in the process of the phenocopy becomes reasonable and even quite probable. On the one hand, this would simply mean that conquest of the environment, besides being considered an extension of the basic assimilatory tendency of life, usually begins with simple trials by phenotypic accommodation or by empirical knowledge. On the other hand it means also that, by virtue of the internal requirements of equilibration, these trials will subsequently give rise to more secure forms of assimilation. These in turn would be ranged in ascending degrees over every level of development, beginning with that of "genetic assimilation" (to retain Waddington's term for the consolidation of mutations by organic selection) or the copy of well-accommodated phenotypes (in other words the reconstruction, if our interpretation of the phenocopy is accepted), and ultimately attaining the various levels of cognitive assimilation, including those of scientific thought.

(II) It is important, however, before seeking equivalents of the phenocopy at the level of intelligence, that some acceptable preliminary generalizations should be made, and their legitimacy agreed upon, which implies, of course, some broadening of our definitions. In what follows, we shall use the phrase "phenocopy in the broad sense" for the replacement of an exogenous formation (phenotypic or cognitive, and due respectively to environmental action or experience of external objects) by an endogenous formation (due to the activities of the organism or the subject). It is here, though, that a generalization must be made. In the case of the biological phenocopy, the endogenous formation which replaces the simple phenotypic adaptation consists of a new genotype, and thus of a form developed within the genome and capable of hereditary transmission. As far as intelligence is concerned, on the other hand, we understand by "endogenous" only those structures which are developed by means of the regulations and operations of the subject. The term endogeneous still seems legitimate, however, since such constructs are not drawn from external objects, but arise from internal logico-mathematical activity engendered by the coordination of the individual's actions. By serving as an assimilatory framework, then, these structures are added to the properties of the external object, but without being extracted from it. Furthermore, beyond the particular level characterized by logic and mathematics (inasmuch as these can be considered "pure"), these endogenous structures will no longer act as a framework for objects (unless they are of a random sort). They will then function deductively, in an exclusively formal manner, a fact which confirms in retrospect their endogenous character.

This extension of the term endogenous is made necessary by two kinds of consideration, both of which are biological in nature. The first is that the structures of intelligence are not innate, and are imposed by necessity only after a long period of construction. There is, certainly, a hereditary factor in the functioning of the intellect, in the sense that no one has ever succeeded in raising the level of an individual's intelligence, either an average individual or a retarded one. On the other hand, however, the structures as such, the general logical relations of transitivity and distributivity for instance, or the group or lattice (combinatorial) structures, are only acquired during a long epigenetic development, in which factors of activity and exercise play as great a part as the maturation of nerve coordinations. In the second place, however, if we may consider logico-mathematical structures as endogenous, it is because they are constructed by the subject, who derives them from the general forms into which his actions are coordinated. These coordinations themselves depend upon nerve coordinations, which are ultimately derived from organic coordinations. In other words, though these constructs may not in fact be hereditary, they nevertheless constitute an extension of organic regulation. Moreover, if they give rise to epigenetic development, which consequently presupposes interactions with date from external sources, they will gradually and precisely replace such interactions with purely internal functioning at the level where formalism and axiomatization no longer depend in any way upon objects.

(III A) In the following discussion, then, it is understood that the term "exogenous," when applied to knowledge, will indicate that it is derived from physical experience. The use of endogenous, when applied to knowledge, will mean that it is due to a logico-mathematical construction. Thus we can proceed to seek, in the cognitive domain, what it is that corresponds to the phenocopy insofar as it involves the replacement of the exogenous by the endogenous. Beginning with the higher levels in order to examine the relations between deduction and experience, we can then return to more elementary levels, and review the problem there as regards the formation of causality and the different kinds of abstraction involved. Once these wide-scale analogies between cognitive situations and those of the phenocopy are established, we can try to show to what extent the relations between exogenous and endogenous factors which characterize the development of knowledge are comparable (and in many cases actually isomorphic in detail) to the relationships between phenotype and genotype which were reviewed in the first part of this study.

On the subject of the apparently general need to replace the exogenous with the endogenous, the entire history of physics provides quite an astonishing case in point. The aim of this discipline, as is generally accepted, is the understanding of the external or material world, which necessarily entails as precise as possible a study and determination of experimental evidence. It thus involves, in the most specific sense of the term, what we just called conquest of the object. In this sense it prolongs the tendency of all organic life to overcome or conquer the environment. Yet even Archimedes, rare among the Greeks in his dedication to experimentation, presented his *Statics* in the form of an axiomatic treatise. We can, to be sure, see that in this he merely imitated the custom of the ancient geometricians, who were obliged as mathematicians to proceed in this way, and who believed moreover that they were describing figures and bodies which existed outside themselves. Yet among present-day physicists who, on the contrary, know well enough that a formalization demands no intuitive obligation whatever, and that axioms can be chosen quite freely provided they meet the necessary and sufficient conditions for a proof, we still find the same concern for axiomatization. A model is set up for examination, which supposedly epitomizes the theory of some particular set of phenomena (of which the details are known only through numerous intricate experiments on, say, temperature and heat). We then find, to our amazement, that this model consists only of definitions, axioms, and theorems incorporating various deductions, as though the physicist was constrained, as if guilty of something, to conceal what he owed to experimentation, and to deceive us into thinking that he had deduced the whole thing. Herein lies the proof, of course, that contrary to the prescriptions of positivism (which were never observed), physics does not restrict itself to description or prediction, but also seeks constantly to understand and to explain. Yet why then does the explanation of objects and the laws which govern them amount to substituting for them mental entities, and reasoning on these as if it were a matter of pure mathematics? Why is it, in other words, that when a discipline deals with knowledge from a clearly recognized exogenous source, this knowledge is treated as if it were purely endogenous?

(III B) The situation becomes clearer if we take into account Lichnerowicz's comparison between theoretical physics and what he terms mathematical physics (in which he is one of the greatest modern specialists). Theoretical physics is concerned with principles and laws verified by experiment, and proposes to justify them deductively by means of precisely the kind of model we have just noted. Mathematical physics is by contrast, according to Lichnerowicz, actually a branch of mathematics. Thus as mathematics has always done when faced with a problem from physics (in the theory of functions or of geometry, etc.), it seeks not to deduce a given truth, but rather to reconstruct it in its totality. More precisely, it attempts by means of purely mathematical construction to reconstitute the set of possibilities of which this particular truth appears to be one of the necessary consequences in the form of a special case.

In such a situation, we begin to understand the reason behind the general substitution of the endogenous for exogenous, and the analogies which this presents to the processes by which the phenocopy is developed. The essential point, in the first place, is that this resort to endogenous reconstruction introduces an element of logical (and therefore intrinsic) necessity into the midst of a system of relationships which before was only locally coherent. There is here from the start an analogy to the phenocopy: namely, when characteristics (the x', y', etc., of chapter 5) are no longer simply the products of interactions between the environment and the synthetic mechanisms, and are replaced by their equivalents, which are due from this point onwards to the syntheses alone, inasmuch as these are directed by the genetic program. There is therefore a transition here from the contingent relationship (environment $\times$ epigenesis) to an internal determination of more necessary character, which could also be said of the transition from exogenous knowledge to a reconstruction which, in a sense, copies it. In the second place, however, this copy (which, we have seen in both cases, is really a reconstruction rather than a copy) arises from the same kind of transposition as far as the successive roles of the external environment or object are concerned. In the case of the phenocopy, the environmental factors x, y, z play a directly causal part, at the level of the phenotype, in imposing the modifications x', y', z' on the course of epigenetic development. But when the corresponding genotype is formed, these external features x, y, z will constitute no more than a joint framework with the modified properties of the internal environment. This framework will itself, in relation to the new genotype, play no more than a selective role, eliminating inadequate mutations and retaining others. If we now return to the construction peculiar to mathematical physics, we find an evident parallel. The mathematician is quite at liberty in the construction of his theory: he knows well enough that its aim is the deductive reconstitution of laws or principles which would elsewhere be imposed experimentally. If he chooses to concern himself with these, it is as a result of the problems he has been set. A selection of interests thus establishes a framework within which his researches are conducted, but a framework without any causal effect upon the process of his deductions. In the third place, if the general teleonomy of this resort to the endogenous is really the pursuit of necessity, then the causal factors determining the detail of the resulting constructions are to be sought, on the cognitive plane as well as on the plane of the biological development of the phenocopy, in those local disequilibriums which persist until the final solution is attained. It is thus, for instance, in the field of physics, that Dirac's delta gave rise to a mathematical elaboration which remained unsatisfactory until the mathematician Schwartz derived from it his elegant theory of distributions.

(IV) Despite these three kinds of general analogy, this overall comparison may still be thought artificial or contrived. In the phenocopy, on the one hand, phenotypic constructions are replaced by more substantial ones associated with the succeeding genotypes; cognitive development, on the other hand, substitutes endogenous constructions for exogenous verification. The correspondence here will undoubtedly appear more convincing if another general indication of it is brought into consideration. Throughout the history of physics, and at every level of psychogenesis, causality has always consisted, in its most general forms, in attributing to objects modes of action modelled upon our own operations or our own logico-mathematical structures. Since the early years of this century, an impressive number of phenomena (from microphysics through crystal theory, etc., to general relativity) seems to have been explained to the extent that a mathematical "group" structure has successfully been conferred upon them. This is not because the physicist holds this structure to be some convenient language by which the facts are better described; the reason is rather that the group structure has served to express the real transformations due to the action of objects conceived of as operators. In other cases structures of order, actions of a probabilistic nature, etc., are similarly attributed to objects, but the general principle of causal explanation remains the same. For systems composed of observable facts and laws, recorded in the manner of exogenous data, inferential systems are substituted, whose structure is that of the subject's operations, and whose elaboration is therefore endogenous. Their attribution to objects thus means that the orderly relationships governing such systems, hitherto simply verified, can in this second phase be deduced by way of necessary compositions of the operational structure invoked. Consequently there is here, once again, a progressive replacement of exogenous knowledge by endogenous construction, and on a very wide scale. When this replacement is not complete, moreover, it can evidently become so, as we can see from each advance in mathematical physics.

It is at the elementary levels of psychogenesis that we begin to find the constitution of causality by attribution of the subject's operations to external objects. We find, for instance, that when faced with the problem of the transmission of movement across a stationary object, seven- to eight-year-olds invent a solution only rarely found in younger children. They suggest that an ''impulse,'' communicated by one moving body, has ''crossed'' the stationary object to set a third one in motion on the other side. This causal explanation thus comes to replace (in the strict sense) an interpretation based upon a simple reading of the facts (as a mere sequence of movements over a certain distance, etc.). It appears at this stage because it is at this level that transitive reasoning ($A \rightarrow B$, $B \rightarrow C$, therefore $A \rightarrow C$) becomes possible; before this, transitivity is not understood. In this case, then, it is this transitivity which is attributed to the three objects involved: the second of them (the stationary one) is in this example ''crossed by an impulse,'' and thus becomes the operator of this transmission. Istances of attributions of other operations can be readily observed. When a piece of sugar is dissolved, comprehension of the conservation of quantity of the then invisible grains will involve the attribution of additive operations. Similarly, when a length of elastic is divided equally into segments, there will be an attribution of distributive operations. When a phenomenon involves an action A and a reaction R, explanation will involve the attribution of coordinated reciprocal actions and their inversions: $\pm A \longleftrightarrow \pm R$ (where $+$ and $-$ are the inversions, and $\longleftrightarrow$ symbolizes the relation of operatory reciprocity). This would only be understood belatedly, because this coordination is not possible before the age of about eleven to twelve.

In an interesting discussion of the concept of explanation or of causal explanation in general,[1] the logician L. Apostel maintains that some truth remains, when all is

---

1. In *L'explication dans les sciences* (*Nouvelle Bibliothèque scientifique*, Flammarion, 1973, pp. 207-214). Reference to the model as ''copy'' is on p. 207.

said, in the positivist interpretation: that all explanation comes down to a description. In some respects, Apostel tells us, an explanatory model is effectively no more than a kind of copy: when we manage to find resemblances between some new fact and phenomena already known to us, such resemblances alone will give us the impression that our understanding is valid. Yet here Apostel makes the point that, in fact, the reason for this eludes our grasp, since a greater degree of generality does not constitute a gain in intelligibility. He goes on to conclude, rather pessimistically, that the reason for intelligibility may not, itself, be intelligible to us. Yet before drawing this somewhat defeatist conclusion, Apostel discusses the suggestion which we have raised here: that causal explanation should be considered as the result of our attribution of our own operations to external objects. However, he does not see this as a satisfactory solution of the problem. Rather, he makes the ingenious objection that, if we say that the actions or interactions of external objects are assimilable to our own operations, we are once again seeking resemblances (or a copy) between facts to be explained and those which are familiar to us or are accessible to our reconstructions. Because of this, he sees no reason why a resemblance between external objects and certain subjective characteristics of the subject should be any more explanatory than a resemblance between two distinct categories of external objects.

These penetrating comments allow us to show precisely how assimilation to an operational model is more explanatory than just any resemblance between two sets of phenomena. At the same time, we can also show how this copy, effected by our own operations, is explanatory precisely because it is more than a copy — because it introduces a replacement or implies a reconstruction, as is also the case, on the biological level, with every phenocopy.

Before causal explanation, the phenomenon to be explained consists, in effect, only of a collection of facts and their relationships or governing laws which have simply been established and in some cases generalized. Such generalizations are, however, extensional in nature, and not productive of structures. It is, in other words, only a matter, in the case of these inductions (passage from the established "some" to the "all" which is anticipated but not yet demonstrated), of exogenous knowledge or its issue. In such a situation, to compare this system of observable data with another set of observables of the same status is, of course, to explain nothing at all. Conversely, however, to assimilate these same facts into an operational structure which, in this second case, is attributed to them is in fact to explain them to the degree that the operations involved maintain relations of necessity among themselves. This will be so, in particular, when the subject can, at least implicitly, make a structure such as a group of transformations (of, for instance, the four-variable group which serves to explain relations of action and reaction) intervene. Such a structure will possess its own laws of composition and closure. Thus it will be explanatory by virtue of combining production and conservation in a necessary way, which is a property common both to causality and to operational constructions. We can therefore hardly accept that intelligibility is incomprehensible. If it cannot be absolute and is always only more or less perceptive, all adequate structuring will nevertheless bring about an advance in intelligibility because adequate structures involve endogenous construction, in opposition to merely exogenous (and therefore empirical) knowledge. Such endogenous constructions are, therefore, necessary inasmuch as they are logico-mathematical, and inasmuch as the logico-mathematical universe engendered by the activities of the subject opens upon the world of the possible and upon the various forms of the infinite. In this way, on at least two fundamental fronts, the logico-mathematical universe transcends the nature of physical objects.

On this basis, then, this explanatory nature of operational models illustrates in the clearest manner the analogy between the replacement of the exogenous by the endogenous — in which this so-called copy of the reality to be explained by the interpretative model consists — and the replacement of the phenotype by a genotype which reconstructs similar characteristics in every biological phenocopy. On the one hand, as we have already seen, exogenous knowledge at the start is comparable to phenotypic reactions in that both are imposed from the outside, whereas the final endogenous reconstruction introduces an element of necessity which corresponds to and transcends[2] the greater stability characteristic of genotypic variations in that they are liable to hereditary transmission. But above all, on the other hand, there is replacement and reconstruction in both cases. This is because during the final exogenous phase the facts and laws established or recorded, despite their being integrated in apparently unchanged form into the final endogenous explanatory model, are not the same whether established or deduced. In fact, in problems of conservation or invariance, the same facts or laws will be profoundly modified, depending upon whether they are simply described or are arrived at by deduction. This was observed, for example, during experiments carried out with B. Inhelder some years ago on the conservation of material quantity and weight when a ball of plasticine was made into a sausage-shape. Where the basic response to such a problem is merely descriptive, the facts and laws involved are not at first anticipated (non-conservative predictions); they can be subsequently foreseen by means of small-scale transformations or established by means of measurement on scales. But insofar as there is no comprehension of their underlying reasons, facts and laws present characteristics only of simple probability, contingency, and non-generality. When, on the other hand, they are operationally deduced,

---

2. Because the necessity belonging to the *a priori* goes well beyond innateness, necessity or apriority characterizes all the more the final closure or completion of a structure, not its preliminary conditions.

a marked contrast appears, recognizable by the use of the three arguments which constantly recur: that nothing has been added or taken away; that the sausage can be made back into the same ball; and a third line to the effect that what is gained in length is lost in width or thickness (this compensatory reckoning being constructed, moreover, before any measurement or verification). The child now finds this conservation so evident and necessary that he is sometimes visibly shocked to be asked such simple and "childish" questions, when a year before he would have answered them quite to the contrary. Such psychogenetic data seem to demonstrate, better than any other example, the essential and often quite rapid opposition which is established between the exogenous phase and the endogenous reconstitution of the same items of knowledge.

7. The Relationship between Exogenous and Endogenous Sources in the Development of Knowledge

It seems, therefore, if the foregoing is valid, that the elaboration of every physical or causal explanation will constitute a cognitive equivalent of the biological phenocopy. Yet one reservation must be noted. It is certainly fundamental that the exogenous processes are the same in nature in both these cases (environmental action or the originating action of external objects). But it is equally true, on the other hand, that the endogenous processes involved are different in their origins. In the case of the biological phenocopy, they arise from the genome, but in the case of the phenocopy's cognitive equivalents, they arise only from the internal self-regulating mechanisms of the individual subject. These mechanisms are themselves, of course, essentially organic in origin. Yet indications of cognitive disequilibrium need not extend as far as the level of the genome in order that stable reequilibration (which thus takes place without the transmission of hereditary characteristics) should occur. We should proceed, then, to examine those formative mechanisms associated with cognitive development, and we had best begin by recalling what we know of the processes of abstraction which are the sources of both our exogenous and endogenous knowledge.

(I A) All new knowledge presupposes an abstraction, since, despite the reorganization it involves, new knowledge draws its elements from some preexisting reality, and thus never constitutes an absolute beginning. Two kinds of abstraction are distinguishable, then, according to their exogenous or endogenous sources; and it is interesting to compare the relationships between them with those existing between the phenotype and the genotype.

In the first place there is the kind of abstraction that we can refer to as empirical, because its information is drawn directly from external objects themselves. The term "simple" (as opposed to empirical) was used in earlier publications, but, as will shortly be seen, this was an exaggerated euphemism. This type of abstraction is exemplified in the case of a subject of any age, who, after weighing a solid object in his hand, is found to retain only his estimation of its weight: other possible results of the action (impressions of the object's color, dimensions, etc.) are disregarded. This first form corresponds, generally, to what we think of as abstraction when the conditions involved are not specified. A second form also exists, however, which is fundamental in that it includes all cases of logico-mathematical abstraction. We can call it ''reflecting abstraction,'' because it is drawn not from objects but from the coordinations of actions or of operations. This form is completely distinct in that it arises from the very activities of the subject: its source is therefore endogenous, which is what interests us here. There are two complementary reasons for the use of the term reflecting abstraction, both resulting from the fact that we are dealing now with the subject himself and no longer with external objects. In the first place, this type of abstraction involves ''reflecting'' in the sense of a physical or geometric projection. In other words, it always implies the ''reflection'' on a higher level of whatever is derived from a lower level. At the level of a two- to three-year-old, for example, there will be the reflection of an action into representation when that action is interiorized. At the level of mathematical thought, there will be reflection when some operation becomes an object of reflexive thought after having until then served only as an instrument of construction. In the second place, however, this reflecting abstraction also involves ''reflexion'' in the sense of a mental reorganization; necessarily so, since reflection culminates on a higher level, where it is a matter first of all of reconstructing what has been abstracted from a lower level in such a way that it is adjusted to the structure of this higher level. Thus the reflection of a set of successive displacements into a representation of them necessitates their reorganization into a system allowing simultaneous evocation of the different parts of the trajectory to be travelled.

The developmental evolution of these two forms of abstraction is quite different. Is is notable in the first place that empirical abstraction, whatever the level involved, never comes into operation by itself. In order to derive information from an object, and even if it can only be drawn from that object, the use of an assimilatory apparatus is indispensable. This assimilatory apparatus is of a mathematical nature: it will involve the relating of one or more classes (or ''schemes'' of action at the sensory-motor level, but these schemes of action are already a kind of practical concept), correspondences, functions, identities, differences or equivalences, and so on. In short, a whole range of instruments is involved which is necessary to the very ''reading'' of experience itself and which is independent of other interpretations which will follow. These recording instruments make possible only the empirical type of abstraction, but it is clear that they themselves are not derived from the object, since they constitute the conditions preliminary to the subject's cognitive grasp of that object. They are thus due to the subject's own activities, and, as such, they arise from previous reflecting abstraction. This will be true, as we have said, even if the empirical abstraction which they make possible subsequently draws its products from the external object alone.

If this is the case as early as the elementary levels of psychogenesis, it is all the more so as the higher levels of scientific thought are approached. In modern physics, a well-contrived experiment presupposes an enormous range of logico-mathematical preliminaries — in the way the problem concerned is approached (that is, in the posing of the question to which nature must answer yes or no), in the construction of relevant apparatus, in the use of measurement in terms of a system of units, and finally in the setting out of results in logico-mathematical language — irrespective of the models and interpretations which these results will later inspire. As a result, the factual data obtained, in that they are provided by the experiment in question, certainly comprise properties of objects and are, in that sense, arrived at by empirical abstraction. Yet this applies only to the content of such experimental data: the form taken by such data is logico-mathematical from the start. It follows that this is so, in fact, from the beginning, but with the qualification that at the most elementary or primitive levels this logico-mathematical form is an extremely simple one. What does remain remarkable is that this characteristic is accentuated as intelligence progresses without science itself ever attaining the empirical content in a "pure" state, which is the same as saying without form.

Before passing on to reflecting abstraction, we should first briefly review this interpretation and note some of its implications. It amounts to maintaining, in short, that there can be no exogenous knowledge except that which is grasped, as content, by way of forms which are endogenous in origin. It should be noted how much this interpretation runs parallel with what has been said concerning phenotypic variations in chapters 2 and 5. No phenotype is possible except as a function of the genotype, and any action of the environment is acceptable only in interaction with the synthetic processes of epigenetic development directed by the genome. When we substitute the terms "empirical experience" for "environment" and "endogenous forms" for "synthetic process," the correspondence becomes quite striking. It breaks down only on the essential point, to which we will return, that the instruments of cognitive assimilation do not extend back as far as the genome, but are directed rather by specifically epigenetic controls. But we must account in detail later on for this single exception to the general parallel between these processes.

(I B) Reflecting abstraction differs in one major respect from the empirical type

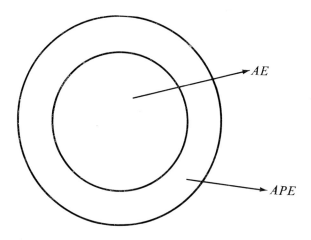

FIGURE 6

Inner circle: characteristics of the object.
Outer ring: characteristics due to the action of the subject temporarily added to those of the object,
and serving as an assimilating frame for reading the characteristics of the object.
EA: empirical abstraction.
PE: pseudoempirical abstraction.

discussed above, in that its development can finally attain a pure state. It alone
supports and animates the immense edifice of logico-mathematical construction.
Its growing power is particularly evident in the continual elaboration of new operations which bear upon those which have gone before (for example, proportions
as relations of relations). Such elaboration is of unlimited fecundity.

But in partial reciprocity with empirical abstraction, which needs reflecting abstraction to function, this latter, in its elementary forms, is accessible to the subject
only when it is embodied in external objects. By itself, of course, this embodiment
does not mean that reflecting abstraction will bear upon those characteristics that
the objects would possess irrespective of the subject such as their weight or size.
On the contrary, the embodiment is merely a matter of temporary characteristics,
introduced and imposed upon the objects by the subject himself — such as the
arrangement of a set of objects into rows or columns — so as to establish that
correspondences involved are nonetheless invariable. In cases such as this, we
can refer to "pseudoempirical abstractions," since there is a reading of the objects
involved, but reading which is really concerned with properties due to the action
of the subject himself (fig. 6). This initial form of reflecting abstraction plays a
fundamental psychogenetic role in all logico-mathematical learning, insofar as the
subject needs to manipulate concrete things in order to understand certain structures which are otherwise too abstract. On the other hand, as we have just seen,
reflecting abstraction in its higher forms can completely free itself from any rela-

tionship with material objects. When this is the case, it gives place to what we may call reflected abstractions (products of the reflecting activity), and to a kind of reflexive thought such as that which animates every formalization.

Thus if the process of empirical abstraction closely recalls, *mutatis mutandis,* that of phenotypic variations, reflecting abstraction, as endogenous construction, is in its turn highly reminiscent of the nature of the genotype. This is so particularly at the elementary levels of pseudoempirical abstraction, where the products of this endogenous activity are embodied in external objects much as every genotype is embodied in its phenotypes. Yet there remain two considerable differences between this cognitive activity (the endogenous source of progressively purified forms) and the formative processes of the genotype. The first, already indicated, is that the development of these higher endogenous structures, which are the most stable cognitive constructs, does not require, in detail at least, programming from the level of the genome. Their development, in other words, depends rather upon self-regulating mechanisms, and though these are certainly of biological origin, they involve no direct recourse to heredity. The second and related difference is that reflecting abstraction culminates by functioning in a pure state. A genotype, on the other hand, would be pure only if it were not embodied in any phenotype, and the "pure genotype" is thus only a theoretical abstraction. Even under laboratory conditions, a strain considered pure is always composed of individuals partially dependent upon the environment in which their epigenesis took place.

(II A) The time has now come to compare organic epigenesis with that of the cognitive functions, to establish how far the differences noted above will still permit the preservation of the same general formative mechanisms. And in this we must pay particular attention to the correspondences between organic phenocopies and their cognitive equivalents. We must also determine, on the other hand, whether the necessity of limiting the field of these cognitive phenocopies will more or less profoundly modify the constructive processes in those domains where only reflecting abstractions intervene.

In more concrete terms, the problem is as follows. The phenocopy is a mechanism which comes into operation, in its strict form, only in cases where a new external environment demands new adaptations. It therefore constitutes, on the organic plane, the most typical instance of equilibration between the organism and an environmental modification. Indeed, if one considers the classic schema of chance mutation and selection "after the event" to be only verbal and abstract (in the sense that it transcends all historical evidence), the phenocopy, seen from our perspective, represents the only instance in which one understands, however poorly, the causal mechanism of this equilibration. Thought of in this way, the phenocopy could intervene (or could have intervened) in every evolutionary situation in which a new adaptation is made necessary by new environmental conditions. Such situations rightfully include the whole range of normal transformations (as opposed to large-scale disruptive mutations which we can consider abnormal) of the world of living things. On the plane of the formation and evolution of knowledge, on the other hand, the influence of the environment (that is, acquiring knowledge of external objects) only constitutes a limited sector. It extends over physical or experimental knowledge in general, and thus over the equilibrium between subject and objects. But the enormous sector of logico-mathematical knowledge is the province of reflecting abstraction alone, and of the equilibrium of systems or subsystems among themselves. Here it becomes evident that the cognitive phenocopy, in the sense of the term used in chapter 6, can only be involved in the first of these two sectors. It will therefore play only a limited role, by constrast with its rightful part in biological evolution. The problem we now come up against is to establish whether this limitation, which appears considerable, produces any profound modification in the unity of the general processes of organic and cognitive construction, or whether we can draw out common elements to show what happens to our basic parallel under these circumstances. This latter effort would involve finding out not only those mechanisms common to both aspects of this general development, but also discovering processes analogous to those of the phenocopy deep in the core of logico-mathematical interventions or progressions where there is no action of objects and which arise only from reflecting abstraction.

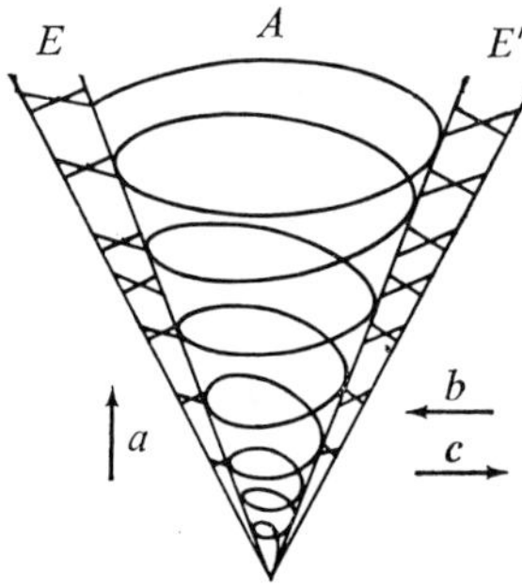

FIGURE 7
Cross section of a reversed cone symbolizing
the epigenesis of cognitive functions.

(II B) With these objectives in mind, we can begin by comparing the processes of organic and cognitive epigenesis to see what becomes, on the cognitive plane, of the three vectors ($\uparrow a$, $\downarrow b$, and $\uparrow c$) with which we were concerned in chapter 5 (in section III-12). On the organic plane, vector $\uparrow a$, it will be remembered, represented the ascending progress of the synthetic processes of epigenetic development. Vector $\downarrow b$ was the downward progress of modifications imposed by the environment and of the resulting disequilibriums whose gradually progressive repercussions sometimes extended right back to sensitize the genes regulating epigenetic development. Vector $\uparrow c$, finally, represented ascending reequilibrations occurring in response to these ($\downarrow b$) disturbances — reequilibrations accomplished by semicontingent and semiexploratory trials involving selection (principally organic selection).

We do find, in the cognitive domain, an analogous form of vector $\uparrow a$, one which is characteristic of successive levels in the hierarchy of cognitive structures. It thus extends through the gamut of cognitive development: beginning with the most elementary innate patterns (nervous and motor coordinations, spontaneous movements and reflexes), it extends through the simpler forms of habit (conditionings and the assimilation of new elements into reflex schemes), through the various circular reactions, the level of sensory-motor intelligence, semiotic and preoperational forms of representation, development of constituent functions and the stage of concrete operations, up to, ultimately, the level of propositional operations. Throughout this development, except at its innate point of departure, there is constant interaction between the endogenous and exogenous processes involved. The endogenous processes will, however, be extended as a result of the constructive effects of reflecting abstraction; the exogenous processes simply represent the utilization of experience. We have noted, however, that reflecting abstraction is eventually capable of functioning in a pure state: it can therefore be represented as a kind of progressively broadening spiral (the central sector A of the inverted cone shown in fig. 7). Interactions with the environment, on the other hand, the province of empirical abstraction and its concomitant reflecting framework, are represented by E and E' in the diagram, and make up the peripheral zone which completely envelops the spiral A.

In the case of vectors $\downarrow b$ and $\uparrow c$, however, we find a degree of difference (though only partial) between their operations in organic and cognitive epigenesis. Vector $\downarrow b$ expresses, in effect, both modifications (x', y', z') imposed by the environment and the disequilibriums (x'', y'', z'') which result from them. We have seen that in the course of organic epigenesis these disequilibriums may prove durable enough to have a sensitizing effect, by the gradual downward encroachment of their repercussions, upon the genes regulating the developmental processes. In cognitive epigenesis, we might therefore imagine a corresponding descent ($\downarrow b$) from higher to elementary stages, ultimately reaching as far as the innate source of these latter stages. But in fact no such correcponding vector is found: on the contrary, in the case of cognitive epigenesis, b vectors follow a direction which is, on the average, horizontal ($\leftarrow$) or only slightly inclined a little below, or even above, the horizontal. Here, in other words, the action of external objects or environmental events has a bearing only upon the endogenous processes (spiral A) of the same level. There may be some repercussion upon the processes immediately below this level (hence the direction $\nwarrow b$) or upon those which represent constructions from it (hence $\searrow b$), but without calling the whole previous construction into question again.

Similarly, the compensatory responses ($\uparrow c$), which in organic epigenesis consist of groping explorations coupled with action upon the environment, naturally show these characteristics reinforced in the case of cognitive development. The exploratory responses on the cognitive level lead to a partial reorganization of endogenous synthesis, and action upon the environment proceeds to the extent that there is complete assimilation and replacement of all exogenous characteristics by an endogenous reconstruction. Examples of this have been noted already in chapter 6 in relation to the cognitive phenocopy. The orientation of these c vectors, however, remains symmetrical with that of the $\underline{b}$ vectors already discussed, that is, on average, it remains horizontal ($\underset{\rightarrow}{c}$).

(III A) This comparison between the two kinds of epigenesis, organic and cognitive, clearly shows how closely they are related. The only exceptional factor in this relationship concerns the formative capacity of the genome itself. On the organic plane, this capacity ends with the development of innate nervous coordinations (as opposed to the acquired patterns of association). But in terms of cognitive development the genome's powers are extended, through a combination of increasingly complex endogenous syntheses (represented by the spiral of fig. 7, since it is by just such a spiral expansion that their cyclic complexity develops). The means of construction for this endogenous expansion is supplied by reflecting abstraction, and by the productive generalizations which derive from it.

If this is the case, then it would seem that some validity attaches to our comparison in chapter 6 between the mechanism of the organic phenocopy and the processes by which initially exogenous knowledge eventually gives place to endogenous reconstructions. These reconstructions effectively reproduce their originals, but give the impression that they have simply copied them (cf. the point made by Apostel, considered in section IV of chapter 6).

It must again be emphasized, however, that these cognitive phenocopies are possible, and conceivable, only in that limited cognitive sector where knowledge is subordinated to the control of experimental fact; in the areas, in other words, that we currently call empirical (as opposed to logico-mathematical), where knowledge depends accordingly upon empirical, rather than reflecting, abstraction. There is here, then, a quite systematic difference between the cognitive and organic spheres of life. Any organic evolutionary change, whether morphogenetic, functional, or physiological, whether macroscopic or biochemical and physical in scale, can only arise in accordance with the environment. In particular, such changes cannot become stabilized without adjustment to the environment, the selective powers of which impose this fundamental limitation. Although, in fact, verification may forever be excluded with respect to the past (and given our state of knowledge, even impossible in the present), we can in principle draw the following conclusions. Every prominent event in the evolution of organized beings could begin — or could have begun — by the development of trial phenotypic accommodations subsequently consolidated, or reconstituted and renewed, by the development of phenocopies. Quite the contrary is true of reflecting abstraction in the cognitive sphere, in that a good portion of its cognitive constructions are utterly alienated from exogenous proofs or knowledge. Thus it follows from this very fact that reflecting abstraction remains completely exempt from the need for any cognitive phenocopy, in the sense of the term we have been using here. Reflecting abstraction, moreover, does not replace empirical abstraction, rather it frames it, as it were, from the outset, and subsequently transcends it infinitely (in the proper sense of the word). Nor does the universe of logico-mathematical possibility replace the real world, but rather engulfs it in order to explain it better. The logico-mathematical sphere is thus a source, but not the actual seat, of phenocopies.

(III B) At this point another analogy, interesting from an epistemological point of view, can be established. The cognitive phenocopy, as we have used the term, signifies the replacement of exogenous knowledge by an endogenous knowledge which reconstructs the original in a similar form. We then find, however, in an even more systematic and necessary way, another analogous mechanism. This mechanism comes into operation when an item of endogenous knowledge from a lower level is reconstructed on a higher level, prior to a reorganization which, by enriching this construct in various ways, will inevitably alter it to some degree. The mechanism of this preliminary reconstruction could be considered homologous rather than simply analogous, since in a biological sense it involves a certain kinship or filiation. The reconstruction in a sense constitutes a replacement, and, in addition, replacement with an obligatory similitude. In this, then, it bears some relationship to the phenocopy, save that here only endogenous knowledge is involved — not items of exogenous information comparable to phenotypic variations. These apparent phenocopies can be termed pseudophenocopies after the pseudoempirical abstractions discussed above. There is all the more reason for this because it is precisely at the level of these pseudoempirical abstractions that this phenomenon of the pseudophenocopy shows its closest resemblance to phenocopies of the exogenous → endogenous type.

We should recall, first of all, the conditions under which reflecting abstraction operates. It begins with the reflection of an endogenous coordination (from any level), so that it may be passed on to the following level. This is the case, for instance, when a sequence of sensory-motor rotations, proceeding step by step in order to rotate an object such as a cube, is raised to the representational level, making it possible to imagine the reverse side of this object when only its usual aspect can be seen. As we have said, though, this reflection first requires a reconstruction. It is one thing to coordinate a sequence of movements, orienting each of them in accordance with equally sequential perceptual indices; it is quite another thing to coordinate the representations of these movements into a simultaneous whole without having actually to carry them out. As a result, the same complex action is not in reality the same when it unfolds on the lower level as when it unfolds on the one immediately above, even though the representation involved will seem to be no more than a faithful copy of the original sensory-motor scheme. In such a case, the initial action and the final representation are both endogenous, in that they arise from the subject's geometry (even though this may be facilitated by the geometry of the object). We can see, therefore, in this reflection and reconstruction quite a close analogy to the exogenous → endogenous type of phenocopy. We can conclude, therefore, that this represents a pseudophenocopy.

This is not, however, the end of this process of reflexive reconstruction: it leads on into a larger-scale reorganization of the whole subgroup of rotatory movements. On the representational level, the subject will thus become capable of coordinating several such rotations, up to the point that he can predict the order of succession and the respective positions of the six faces of the cube as it is turned one way or another. The compositions of this subgroup turn out to be tedious to master right off by deductive means, however, and one finds that young subjects still need to base their deductions on partial manipulations of objects for quite some time. In such cases, the subject proceeds by a reading (from the object itself) of the results of his endogenous coordinations, and this, therefore, represents what we earlier termed pseudoempirical abstraction. Subsequently, though, this reading is followed by the subject's liberation with regard to these pseudoempirical forms of ascertainment: internalized deductive thought then occurs in its own right, without external support. We consequently find, between this latter phase and that of the pseudoempirical coordinations, a new relationship of replacement and reconstruction — a new case, in other words, of a pseudophenocopy.
This process seems, in fact, to be very widespread throughout the whole area of logico-mathematical thought. The whole stage of concrete operations (between the ages of 7-8 and 11-12), before propositional operations and their combinations permit the beginnings of hypothetical-deductive thinking, is characterized by such passages from pseudoempirical abstraction to operational deduction, with a progressively greater freedom from the need for actual manipulation of objects.
Even at the heart of scientific thought analogous mechanisms are again discovered amid constructions based upon the pure reflecting abstraction of the mathemati-

cian. We can distinguish two successive stages here: in the first, some structure is used implicity in the mathematician's chief operational compositions, but in the subsequent stage this structure is teased out and gives rise to a theory. Comparing these stages, we can establish that a psychological change has taken place much as follows: operations which, at the earlier stage, served essentially as instruments of calculation or deduction, have become, at the latter stage, differentiated objects of thought in their own right. It is this kind of "thematization" with explicit taking of consciousness [*prise de conscience*] and what we have called reflected abstraction (or reflexive and retrospective thought), which allows the construction of a new theory. It directly becomes apparent that the same relationship between replacement and reconstruction, characteristic of the pseudophenocopy, is found between the operation as a simple instrument and the same operation as a "thematized" object of reflexive thought. Here again both terms in this relationship are purely endogenous coordinations. The pseudophenocopy will therefore appear in the interval, as it were, before reflexion (which brings about reorganization) produces more or less considerable enlargement of this new theory. The first condition of the theory's development was thus the "reflecting" with all the aspects of the phenocopy which came along with it.

All in all, what we have called the cognitive phenocopy involves a mechanism quite general in its occurrence, since this involves the replacement of exogenous knowledge by a faithful endogenous reconstruction. The analogy with what happens on the organic level when a phenotypic variation gives place to genotypic production of a similar form seems clear enough. It is true that if strictly defined (as a sequential relationship between exogenous and endogenous formations) a mechanism such as this must be restricted to those cases where knowledge emanates initially from experience; where knowledge is acquired, in other words, from the action of objects or of the physical environment upon the subject's coordinations. And since there exists a vast region of cognitive construction which is purely endogenous (represented by logico-mathematical operations due solely to reflecting abstraction), this is in fact an important limitation of the range of the cognitive phenocopy. Yet despite this, the mechanism involved is nonetheless of interest and importance, since it represents a particular case of a much more widespread mode of construction, linked with all processes of reflection and reflexive reconstitution. And if, regarding this considerable extension of the process, there continues to be a notable difference between organic and cognitive processes, then there is an evident and natural reason for this. In the organic sphere, no form can ever be dissociated from its content, whereas the proper function of cognitive processes, on the contrary, is to construct forms, then forms of forms, and so on. These constructs will be ever more abstract, and freer or more detachable from all content.

8. The Problems of Equilibrium

I must hope to be excused for returning, at the close of this study, to general comparisons between organic and cognitive processes, especially as these were the subject of the earlier book *Biology and Knowledge*. But the fact remains that the questions we have just been examining — those concerning phenocopies and the still more general processes which are their analogues — do suggest some new areas of common ground between the territories of biology and epistemology. And I believe that a great many of the relationships existing between these two domains arise from the fact that processes of equilibration, by means of self-regulating mechanisms, are common to both.

(I A) If our interpretation is valid, the explanation of the phenocopy is best sought in the disequilibriums (or the instability of equilibrium) resulting from the occurrence of a phenotypic variation. Such a variation occasions an opposition, or a kind of conflict, between the requirements of an unaccustomed or altered environment and those of the processes of epigenetic development directed by a hereditary program. The resulting disequilibriums, which in some cases will end up sensitizing the genes regulating epigenisis, will then trigger off a process of reequilibration, which will take the form of mutations directed to the zone of disequilibrium. These mutations, in turn, channelled by processes of selection (effected by the external framework, but principally by the internal environment) will ultimately take on forms analogous to those of the phenotypic forms. This whole process would, therefore, be directed by a general mechanism of disequilibration and reequilibration, and we find this at work once more in the cognitive phenocopy. In that case as well, exogenous knowledge, because it lacks internal necessity and because the extent of its generality is unknown, will maintain a latent disequilibrium, especially when the observable facts involved have only been discovered or analyzed with difficulty because they were unforeseen. Subsequently this disequilibrium will lead to a reequilibration by means of endogenous reconstruction. This process will proceed to the extent that the empirical findings can be assimilated to a deductive pattern of operations (sensitized by the disequilibrium those findings have produced). The deductive operations will then be attributed to the objects whose actions, until then, remained poorly understood.

The first thing to be noted here is that these disequilibriums and reequilibrations, which characterize organic or cognitive phenocopies, arise in both cases from the first of three categories which are readily distinguished among the general processes of equilibration. But this first category is of necessity linked to the other two. As in every case where a system is both cyclic and partially open (cf. in chapter 1, the scheme $A \times A' \rightarrow B... Z \times Z' \rightarrow A$), the categorization is as follows: first, equilibrium between the internal elements of the system $(A, B... Z)$ and external elements $(A', B'... Z')$; second, equilibrium between subsystems of the same or neighbouring ranks; third, equilibrium between these subsystems and the overall system, or other in words, between differentiation and integration. What is striking here is the extent to which the problems thus raised are found to correspond in detail when biological and epistemological questions are compared. As far as these questions themselves are concerned (though there will be progressive differences in their solutions), the correspondence seems to stand almost term for term.

We should first briefly recall what we have said elsewhere concerning this question in a cognitive context. Having done this, we can then try to translate the various elements of this analysis into biological terms. The starting point of processes of equilibration is, naturally, evident in the subject's earliest sensory-motor actions when he attempts to reproduce or generalize these actions, and when he seeks to apply the scheme of these actions to a multiplicity of objects. This will happen subsequently with representative schemes or concepts, with functions, and, finally, with operational schemes. In all these cases, wherever there is interaction between the properties of external objects (imposed by experience) and the subject's endogenous activities, there will be an equilibration of these exchanges. And there are at least five questions raised by this equilibration for which we find equivalents in the sphere of organic development.

(I B) First there is the question of the necessary equilibrium between the assimilation of objects to a scheme of actions or operations, whatever its level, and the accommodation of this scheme to the objects. This accommodation may be temporary or lasting; and its result may be either a greater or lesser modification of the scheme itself or, alternatively, conservation and final completion of its original properties. This accommodation may, again, be more or less rapid and direct; or it may develop only tentatively, more or less parallel with corresponding biological situations. For cognitive assimilation is itself also a process of integration, and to cognitive accommodation there will thus correspond, according to this organic parallel, either unstable phenotypic accommodations or stable hereditary adaptations. Yet there continues, meanwhile, to be one important difference that threatens this apparent parallel. It is a property of cognitive mechanisms to dissociate

form and content. Once these forms with their characteristic operational structures are disengaged, they can no longer be contradicted by the external objects to
which they may be applied. Thus a quasi-permanent accommodation is set up
which can no longer be modified except by its differentiation and completion. This
disparity would pose a grave threat to the parallel we have been elaborating were
it not for two further considerations: first, that the elementary stages of comport-
ment and of representation furnish all transitions between extreme states; second,
that succession of reflecting abstractions shows that the origin of logico-mathematical structures is essentially endogenous and thus initially organic. The equilibrium between subject and objects (which is ultimately an equilibrium between
mathematics and reality) thus takes on a different aspect. It no longer appears to
be of a nature distinct from the equilibrium between the organism and its environment, but, on the contrary, as the ultimate realization of a harmony sought at
every level. The development of this harmony is constantly opposed by the environment insofar as this environment remains limited and continually presents new
and unforeseen difficulties. But this equilibrium becomes realizable when this environment is expanded indefinitely by the power of thought so as to include the
whole universe of possibility.

Hence, however, our second problem, that of the "norm of reaction" which expresses the limited number of possible variations open to a genotype when it is
confronted by a wide range of values in an environmental variable. This is an
expression, in other words, of the genotype's flexibility, and of its richness in
terms of the production of phenotypes. To this will correspond, in cognitive
terms, the "norm of accommodation" of a scheme of cognitive assimilation. We
find here, once again, that the parallel between the organic and cognitive notions
is close as far as the elementary cognitive phases are concerned. But when we
come to later developments, the norm of accommodation of a cognitive scheme
will no longer be simply a measure of its own flexibility, but rather of the number
of interactions and coordinations it has been able to enter into with other schemes.
Here, once more, there is the beginning of a disparity between the cognitive and
the organic. The various genotypes of a species are incapable of coordination
among themselves except as a result of genetic recombination. Nor do they
constitute a totality whose elements can function simultaneously or by turns, as do
the various schemes of a system whose organization depends upon reciprocal assimilations. And from this disparity there comes the increasing difference between
organic norms of reaction and cognitive norms of accommodation.

(I C) A third question is that posed by a changed environment. In cognitive terms,
the corresponding situation arises when a scheme or system of schemes is
confronted with new objects or a new experimental situation. Here, yet again, we

find deep-seated analogies, but also a number of differences which stem from the fact that, whereas organic reactions are essentially successive or sequential (this being a function of their developmental history), it is possible for knowledge to embrace a range of simultaneous comparisons. This range becomes progressively wider by virtue of memory and because the new structures involved become coordinated with previously formed structures which still remain current. In short, then, knowledge is extended in this way because it leads to a general conservation of its schemes. The result in terms of organic development, when environmental change occurs, is that the possible responses are broadly reduced to three: non-survival because of a failure to adapt; the development of phenotypic adaptations for which there will be no genotypic replacements; or the development of pheno-copies. A further possibility, of course, would be the appearance of purely fortui-tous mutations, with selection "after the event": but this is, at best, the least likely solution of the problem. We have already seen that cognitive analogues of these organic possibilities take the form of simple and unstable accommodations, of cognitive phenocopies or pseudophenocopies. But there is also an additional possibility, and one which is frequently realized. Before the operational recon-struction which succeeds any provisional accommodation and even before the latter is produced, in some cases the new experimental situation will not yet give rise to any construction at all. The subject, meanwhile, has already provided him-self with constructions applicable to objectively analogous situations, but he does not see the possibility of generalizing from these. There is thus a staggered or out of phase effect in time, in that structures already accessible (say, for instance, conservation of the quantity of matter in an object when its shape is changed) are not yet applied to new content (for instance the conservation of the object's weight). These staggered effects, so common in the course of development, are therefore relative to the relations between cognitive forms and their content. They demonstrate once more how difficult it is to dissociate and generalize these forms. In comparative terms, they are part of a general process which goes beyond the organic level where form and content remain much more closely linked. The only exception is in the development of the nervous system, but this is in any case integral to the development of conduct.

The fourth question concerns, again, the cognitive version of the phenocopy. What we have called the cognitive phenocopy is a process which ensures a ready transition between simple objective verifications (or practical successes) and the operational reconstruction which ensures their understanding. There is a corres-ponding duality, in biological phenomena, between the unstable phenotypic varia-tion and the subsequent genotypic reconstruction which attains equilibrium. The fact remains, however, that pseudophenocopies appear very commonly in the course of cognitive development, concomitant with the endogenous construction of successive forms which take no account of the object's properties, nor, therefore, of empirical content. The existence and abundance of pseudophenocopies shows once more the novelty which comes with this liberation of form from content on the level of knowledge.

We come, finally, to the fifth question raised by simple equilibrium between subject and objects, or between the endogenous and exogenous elements of a cognitive systems (the first of the three general categories of equilibrium we distinguished above). This last question concerns the fundamental problem of affirmation and negation. Any cognitive equilibrium (and the same will apply to equilibrium between subsystems, and between their differentiation and integration into a totality with its own laws) will effectively incorporate as many negative as positive features. One object will be opposed to others which differ from it, one action to others with different characteristics. Progress towards an objective will imply distancing from the starting point — the addition of elements at one point will involve their subtraction from another, and so on. One reason, in fact, for the systematic disequilibriums that we observe in the initial stages of cognitive development is that the subject begins on all fronts by centering himself on positive characteristics and disregarding the negative. He will, for example, judge the length of two trajectories by comparing their points of arrival without reference to points of departure, which thus omits the comparison of intervals and renders the evaluation merely ordinal, or even semiordinal. Again, he will not understand a particular conservation because he is centered on what is added in one dimension (length, for instance), thus failing to see that this addition is balanced by an equivalent subtraction in another dimension (width). The subject will subsequently discover a number of negative aspects which had hitherto escaped him; but it is only at a later operational stage, at the age of 7-8, that he will manage to relate these negatives (necessary to logical coherence) to positive aspects in any systematic way.

Equivalents to this cognitive negation are found from the earliest of organic reactions onwards, and stages can be distinguished in their development which correspond, more or less, to those we can observe on the behavioral and representational levels. The most elementary cognitive form of negation is in fact a negation imposed from outside, which the subject is therefore obliged to accept. The failure of some attempt or trial, or the discovery of facts which contradict expectation, these would be among the earliest examples of this kind of negation, since here the subject undergoes the negative operation more or less consciously, rather than having to construct it himself. The biological equivalent of this exogenous negation is the opposition or rejection of a particular variation by the environment, which can begin with the initial phenotypic variations if these show a degree of variability before being selected. This kind of exogenous negation will operate in cases where selection is entirely restricted to a filtering process due to the environment. As soon as selection is oriented towards choice, on the other hand, even if the choices involved relate to nothing but external situations, a new form of negation appears. Such choices naturally involve, as complements or correlates to their positive aspects, negations by which some conditions will be discarded or simply fail to be retained. A supplementary advance is achieved when this rejection is no longer related only to some factor in the environment (as for instance when the best conditions for building a nest are chosen). Instead, when trial variations come to correspond with selective procedures involving choice, the organism will manage to discard some trials in order that others may be retained. There comes, however, a decisive turning point in the development of biological negation before it becomes cognitive (although frontiers between the organic and cognitive themselves become gradually blurred in the area of behavior, even when, as with instincts, such behavior is programmed by heredity). This turning point appears at the stage of transition from selection in accordance with the external environment to selection which is internal or organic. At this point the negation no longer takes the form of some local or fortuitous rejection; rather, it becomes correlated, in a sense, with the positive operation which is its complement. We become concerned, in other words, with the systematic process of inhibition which necessarily accompanies all activation. This is comparable, then, to the cognitive level at which negations are no longer simply imposed from outside, but begin to be constructed by the subject himself. It is self-evident, however, that this system of interdependent activation and inhibition is primarily a characteristic feature of the endogenous processes of epigenetic synthesis. It plays a further part in the equilibrium between organism and environment, but only indirectly. Meanwhile, the new problems which this has raised must lead us to consider the other two general forms of equilibrium; and these will inevitably extend the significance of the first.

(II A) When a phenocopy is developed, the initial phenotypic variation is not sufficient to ensure a stable equilibrium. The achievement of this is left to the final genotype, although the forms that this reconstructs will appear very similar to that of the initial somatic modification concerned. If this is the case, it follows that this equilibrium must effectively ensure a complete compatibility, not only with the external environment, but also with those endogenous mechanisms which collectively subject every new variation to a process of organic selection.

This leads us back to the second broad category of equilibrium, a type which is common to all cognitive systems as well as to all organic totalities, namely, internal equilibrium between subsystems which are differentiated deep within these larger overall systems. This involves a fundamental process from the cognitive standpoint, because this equilibrium is far from being established automatically as soon as the subject has succeeded in elaborating such subsystems. A well-known example, in subjects up to the age of 7-8, is that of the conflicts possible (of which many kinds can be observed) between the spatial and numerical properties of objects. When, for instance, objects whose unequal elements can be aligned to give a length or can be counted to give a number are given to a young subject, he can perform either of these operations correctly; but nevertheless he soon runs into difficulty. He forgets the inequality of the elements he is counting and, starting with the idea that the same number must correspond to the same length (which would be reasonable if the elements were equal), he becomes entangled in all kinds of contradiction. Difficulties of a comparable kind in the coordination of two systems of reference can also be observed at higher levels of cognitive development.

Equilibrium between a cognitive scheme (or group of schemes forming a subsystem) and its objects presupposes the harmonization of assimilations and accommodations, these being imposed here by the properties of the objects involved. In exactly the same way, the equilibration of two or more subsystems will depend upon the interplay of reciprocal assimilations and accommodations. This question of reciprocal assimilation does not, of course, lead to the identification of the subsystems concerned; but it does allow us to sort out correspondences between them, and to note any mechanisms which they have in common. Their reciprocal accommodation, on the other hand, leads us to recognize the differences between them and, therefore, to construct an interplay of complementary or correlative partial negations of the positive characteristics.

We must also take account here of what happens when one subsystem is at a higher level than another in a hierarchy where the one is placed directly above the other. In terms of their relationship, the result will not be that the higher subsystem is reduced to the lower simply because it has engendered new characteristics. Nor will the reverse reduction occur, provided the lower subsystem conserves its existence and maintains its own characteristics, however limited these may be. In such cases, therefore, the relationship is again one of reciprocal assimilation and accommodation. There is thus no need for the equilibrium involved to be specially categorized; unless, of course, the lower subsystem becomes completely integrated in the higher, thus forming a distinct element in some new overall totality. In that case it will conform to the third general type of equilibrium distinguished above.

This third type raises further interesting problems from the cognitive standpoint, and these must again be pointed out before we pass on to consider organic parallels. This type is best described as an equilibrium between differentiation and integration: it develops, not between one subsystem and other associated subsystems, but between the particular subsystem and the encompassing totality of which it forms a part. This at once raises a question with an evident biological as well as an epistemological significance. Once these subsystems are coordinated among themselves, with no further conflict or contradiction, then an encompassing overall system will sooner or later take shape around them. Why, we may ask, does this kind of overall system emerge? Such a totality will not only be quite distinct from its constituent subsystems, but must also fulfil a twofold condition of equilibrium: it must not interfere with the differentiation of subsystems within it, and at the same time it must maintain its own existence and unity of integration despite this degree of internal differentiation. Such overall systems are certainly a feature of cognitive development: new ones are often elaborated, for example, in the conspicuously constructive discipline of mathematics. There comes to mind, for instance, current research on categories which has revived interest in earlier work on structures carried out by members of the Bourbaki group.

These overall systems generally have three fundamental characteristics: they have their own laws of composition, independent of the properties of their constituents; they provide underlying reasons for whatever is demonstrable or observable (but remains unexplained) at the level of these constituent elements; and they have the capacity to develop new content in such a way as to compensate for the effect of the general law of inverse proportion between the extension of ideas and their comprehension. An example from mathematics would be the addition of negative whole numbers to the natural numbers N. These latter only have a "monoid" overall structure, but when the negative whole numbers are added as a new content, this permits construction of an overall group structure whose elements are the whole numbers Z. Generalization, by division, then leads to rational numbers (Q) and to real numbers (R), represented by hierarchically included structures which first take the form of "rings," then that of "bodies." And we find, in fact, that every situation in such a progression develops new laws of totality, the reasons for previous systems and the new contents widening the extension of even those totalities richest in properties. Creative progressions such as these attain a spectacular scale at the level of scientific thought; yet similar mechanisms forming coherent overall systems can in fact be observed as early as the operatory levels of psychogenesis.

This applies well enough to cognitive development, but we must proceed no further without reference to its biological equivalent. Our interpretation of the phenocopy will make sense only insofar as both the latent disequilibriums and corresponding reequilibrations, by releasing or triggering mutations, imitate the previous somatic forms insofar as this corresponds to mechanisms essential to all organic life. We have referred repeatedly here to the following three general categories of equilibrium: (1) the internal equilibrium and, therefore, the system of regulations

belonging to each of the levels of the successive epigenetic syntheses, from elementary intracellular relations to tissues and organs; (2) equilibrium of interregulations, which ensures close liaison or interdependency between levels placed one
above the other in the hierarchy: this connects, therefore, those varieties of equilibrium between subsystems which occur generally in organic life, and is at the
same time directed towards the third type; (3) the equilibrium of the organism as
a totality, which involves a functional solidarity (not just a compromise, as it so
often is the case in the course of cognitive psychogenesis) between differentiation
and integration.

This system, taken as a whole, implies much more than is often referred to as the
"total potentiality" of the genetic possibilities of the genotype considered. This is
because this total potentiality involves not only a complex system rich in possible
activations, but also complementary regulation of inhibitions. This latter is called
for, of course, by virtue of the universal and necessary relationship between positive and negative features, which we have already discussed. The essential interdependence of the activating and inhibitory factors must therefore imply, obviously enough, general regulation which encompasses the whole epigenetic system as
much as the genome itself. And it is this which should allow us to understand the
sensitization of the regulating genes in cases where disequilibrium is propagated from its
beginning in the phenotypic variations imposed by the environment.

(III) This comparison between organic and cognitive processes of equilibration
can be taken further. But to establish correspondences between the phenocopies
that occur in such apparently separate domains requires one more rapprochement
regarding those behavorial reactions which compensate for external perturbations.
When some unforeseen factor arises which prevents an action from achieving its
goal or contradicts the expectation or generalization of a scheme, we can then in
fact distinguish three phases in the successive equilibrations which this brings
about. In human subjects, these phases develop as stages, between the ages of 4-5
and 11-12. First comes an elementary stage (referred to elsewhere as conduct α [1])
which is characterized by the subject's attempts to cancel the disturbance alto-
gether: a troublesome object will be eliminated or modified, an undesirable fact
denied or distorted, and so on. The second phase, on the other hand, is one of
compromise or attempted integration (conduct β): the prior scheme is accommo-
dated by minimal alterations or more extensive differentiation, but a duality
between the internal and external factors involved is still maintained. During the
last stage (conduct γ) complete integration is finally achieved: the modification,
which was originally only an external disturbance, has ultimately become incorpor-

---

1. In the forthcoming study *L'équilibration des structures cognitives*.

ated into the system of transformations as a possible variation. As such it is not only predicted by the system but henceforth is part of the system's own laws of composition. In other words, what was at first a compensation to reestablish an equilibrium unbalanced by external disturbance, has become a positive transformation at the heart of an improved equilibrium. It is obvious, of course, that this kind of cognitive development (stages α to γ) does not simply consist of an internalization of the initial external disturbances concerned. If it did, we might imagine that this was simply a case in which ultimate operations had been derived from external objects (by empirical abstraction), and that these operations were therefore nothing but copies of established modifications. On the contrary, this integration of the disturbance into the system, in the form of internal variations, implies that an endogenous reconstruction has taken place. And it follows that what we are dealing with, in cases such as this, are in fact varieties of cognitive phenocopy.

We can, as was suggested, relate these findings to the development of the organic phenocopy and once more discern the analogy involved. As a result we learn more about the kind of functional inventiveness which the organic phenocopy brings to its relationship with the environment. At points where the environment plays or may still play a disruptive role (cf. phase α above), the immediate response of the phenotypic variation is one of active compromise (phase β); the stable genotypic variation then transforms what was initially a perturbation into new and positive properties which become part of a hereditary program (phase γ). But more than this is involved, and we may wonder whether in fact a more general property of self-organizing biological systems is not at work here. In a study of the relations between information theory and biology,[2] the biophysicist H. Atlan seeks to justify neo-Darwinist ideas on the role of chance. In the process he actually modifies these ideas profoundly; but this is a topic to which we will return in the concluding chapter. Atlan summarizes his thesis as follows: "The self-organizing systems are not only resistant to noise (collectively, the random hostilities of the environment), but actually make use of it to the extent that they transform it into an organizational factor."[3] As will be seen, this inversion of meaning corresponds quite strikingly to that by which external perturbations (conduct α) become variations within the system (conduct γ) in the cognitive process which we have just recalled. And this of course has been summed up already, by H. V. Foerster, in the well-known phrase "from noise to order."

---

2. H. Atlan, *L'organisation biologique et la théorie de l'information* (Paris: Hermann, 1972).

3. [Les systèmes auto-organisateurs, non seulement résistent au bruit (ensemble des agressions aléatoires de l'environnement) mais parviennent à l'utiliser jusqu'à le transformer en facteur d'organisation.]

(IV) We have still to deal, finally, with the process of maximizing equilibration[4] which is of such central importance in cognitive development. Here again we must ask whether an organic equivalent is to be found. In cognitive terms, this type of equilibration comes about as a response to disturbance, which may be positive (contradiction, etc.) or negative (blanks or gaps in data). The ensuing compensation tends not simply to return to the former state, but to go beyond it in the direction of the best possible equilibrium compatible with the situation. There are many reasons for this, but they all arise directly, by and large, from the fact that knowledge derives from action, and that schemes of action are schemes of assimilation which aim at the integration of objects into structures (or coordinations of schemes) so that they can then be utilized and understood. Thus the original core of this development is functional, and it is best seen in terms of two inseparable aspects. Cognitive assimilation consists essentially in action upon objects: its function is not to copy these objects, but rather to transform them or place them in a framework (by the establishment of relationships or correspondences between them by categorization, and so on). It therefore embodies a constant twofold tendency: first, to extend the field of its assimilations, and second to enrich the comprehension of this field. Thus on one hand the aim is that every cognitive scheme should assimilate the greatest possible number of elements, and on the other that these elements should be more sharply differentiated by the establishment of new relationships which extend those already developed.

As regards the mechanisms by which this progressive development is made possible, they naturally are also bipolar. (And nothing, by the way, can be more astounding than the speed and scale of cognitive acquisition during the first eighteen months of life, even though a human child has only sensory-motor instruments at his disposal prior to the acquisition of language.) On the one hand, there is learning as a function of experience with the empirical abstractions which make it possible. But on the other hand there is also reflecting abstraction; and this (as we have seen in chapter 7), from the first coordinations of actions or schemes, permits the derivation from those coordinations of new assimilatory frameworks and new structures by combining reflection onto new cognitive levels with reorganizing reflexion. What we have said about pseudophenocopies (chapter 7, section III B) provides an example of this kind of enrichment or enhancement, which develops through the channel of pseudoempirical and reflective abstractions, and of the maximizing equilibration which is its result.

The problem, though, is to ascertain whether these interpretations, which seem almost self-evident in their cognitive application, are capable of faithful and credible translation into terms of organic development. There are in fact a number of

---

4. [l'équilibration majorante].

reasons which force us to admit the existence of such maximizing equilibrations in the evolution of life itself. There is first a quite definite convergence between the analysis of cognitive developments just sketched and what some contemporary biologists call progress. In using this term, of course, they are seeking to give an objective content to a quite old-fashioned idea in reaction against the speculative excesses of the earliest evolutionary theorists. Thus as criteria of evolutionary progress Julian Huxley, for instance, invokes an increasing control of the environment by the organism and a gradual accompanying growth in the independence of the organism from environmental influence. Rensch's ideas on the subject are oriented in the direction of increased "opening," in the sense of an expansion of the possibilities of adaptation. There is also the fact that an examination of organic development does reveal mechanisms which correspond, in a sense, to the part played by reflective abstraction in cognitive development. In both cases the constituent elements involved are drawn from previous levels in order to give place at a subsequent level to a reconstruction which differentiates and goes beyond them. We have referred to this general phenomenon elsewhere as convergent reconstruction and extension,[5] and though it includes the obvious homologies, its range is in fact wider. In the case of a homologue, the same system of organs (the four-limbed skeleton, for example, in birds and mammals) becomes gradually diversified in the course of its descent; whereas convergent situations imply that a long and unknown path must have been followed from remote common origins. In both cases, however, a reconstruction that makes use of earlier materials[6] culminates in advances in adaptability. There is, finally, a third general reason in support of maximizing equilibration as an organic phenomenon. This rests on the fact that the transformation of organs is almost always connected with new patterns of behavior or new reactional variations. And since all behavior is teleonomic, it is difficult to attribute ends to such processes other than those tending to improvement or progress, however modest such advances may be.

In each of these cases again, therefore, we find that phenomena we have pointed out in the sphere of cognitive development recur analogously in the organic sphere. The organism acts constantly upon its environment instead of merely submitting to it. And this action, again, entails in varying degrees a twofold advance: in extension and in comprehension. Extension involves an enlargement of the environment with trial adaptations in sectors as yet unoccupied; comprehension involves an enhancement or enrichment of properties, or of possibilities for variation and for "opening."

---

5. [reconstructions convergentes avec dépassements].

6. The utilization of earlier materials does not imply that every case of homology rests on the action of the same genes: this has been shown to be quite untrue as a generalization. But this in no way excludes wider structural relationships relative to the systems of genetic regulation.

9. General Conclusions

The preceding study rests upon two hazardous hypotheses. The first is that there is a certain generality in the process of the phenocopy, as if all new adaptation began with phenotypic explorations or trials and was not the result, as the simplistic doctrine in fashion would have it, of numerous chance events sorted out by later selections. The second hypothesis suggests a close relationship between organic and cognitive phenocopies; and its implication is that the properties of equilibration and self-regulation, recurring in all spheres of life, denote the existence of a general tendency towards the endogenous reconstruction of unstable exogenous acquisitions.

These two theses are closely linked. Both appear to stem from a very basic fact which some writers have emphasized, but which is not always accorded its due importance. This is, simply, that in animals, evolutionary transformations of adaptive significance (not, therefore, just any mutation) are closely bound up with new patterns of behavior. In plants, we tend not to speak of behavior because the reactions involved are not quick enough (though a speeded-up film would serve to reestablish the relationships concerned); instead, we confine ourselves to terms such as reactional variation. Here, though, it is understood that "reactional" implies a compensatory activity on the part of the organism. It is not merely a tautological synonym for adaptive, because adaptation, according to official doctrine, may be the passive result of chance variations being subjected to externally imposed processes of selection.

Taking animals first, it is quite evident that from the most primitive invertebrate levels upwards there is a constant correlation between the morphology and the behavioral patterns of any species we may study. The amœbae, for example, make use of their transient pseudopodia, while the flagellates rely on permanent flagella. Species with radial symmetry lie passively in wait for their food, while those with bilateral symmetry go in search of it (unless the adult forms are anchored, as are oysters or mussels, and use other appropriate methods). Cephalopods and arthropods show innumerable distinct patterns of behavior relative to their morphologies. Fishes swim, birds fly, and man himself owes a good deal of his intelligence to his hands.

All this presents us, then, with one general problem. Must we accept, in the first place, that all these specialized organs were formed independently from the patterns of behavior that they subsequently entailed? Can we agree, in other words, that such organs — and perhaps even part of the associated behavior — were entirely the product of successive chance occurrences coupled with subsequent selection? The alternative would be to accept, not necessarily that the formation of such behavior came before that of the organs, but that both were begun and then developed by obligatory interaction. Our own modest example of such an interaction would be that of *Limnaea,* changing shape in relation to its movements. Can we say, though, that this is the more acceptable view?

There are, of course, classic objections to the doctrine of chance and selection which have never been adequately refuted. A notable instance concerns the considerable number of mutations, distinct but related to one another, which must be invoked to explain the formation of any kind of differentiated organ. But setting such objections aside, there remain a number of further arguments which tend to support the hypothesis that conduct does play an active causal role.

We should recall, first of all, that reactions to the environment are a widespread and generally observed feature throughout ontogenesis (hence, of course, the relevance of paedogenesis, which was considered in chapter 3 and need not be returned to here). Every animal from the beginning of its life is effectively engaged in constructive conduct. As regards the more lowly species, we need only look back to figure 3 in chapter 1 for an illustration of the effects of environmental change during growth. In more advanced species, the importance of play and exploratory activities proper to childhood is well enough appreciated. J. Monod tells us that all evolution is the result of troublesome disturbances or imperfections which disturb "that very conservation mechanism which is uniquely the advantage" of living things. But in saying this, he surely overlooks his own ontogenesis. Are we to understand that, instead of preserving unchanged the characteristics which came with his birth, a series of unfortunate accidents has made him a Nobel Prize winner? His judgment concerning evolution is made yet more curious when, in an excellent passage, he himself underlines the part played by behavior, referring to one of the most decisive turning-points in the development of the vertebrates. If tetrapod vertebrates exist, Monod tell us, it is "because a primitive fish chose to explore the land, even though it could only move about on it by skips and hops."[1] There are a number of possible reactions to this decisive remark. We may choose, first, to see the amusing reference to youthful patterns of behavior: if this were an elderly fish, it must have remained very young at heart to attempt

---

1. [parce qu'un poisson primitif "a choisi" d'aller explorer la terre, où il ne pouvait cependant se déplacer qu'en sautillant] *Le hasard et la nécessité,* p. 142.

such an adventure. But the main point is one which does not involve any such liberty with Monod's own terms. A fish that decides to establish itself on land (contrary to all innate patterns of behavior, even if it happened to be one of the Dipnoi) is obviously capable only of explorations at a phenotypic level;[2] more stable modes of action must await the development of genetic variations. It seems, therefore, that an appeal to behavioral factors leads implicity to the recognition of a certain generality in the phenocopy, but we will come back to that presently. For the moment we need only note that such references to behavior should be understood as conveying all manner of restless seeking out and conquest of new territory by virtue of the general need to feed schemes of action. And such patterns of behavior have their beginnings at least as early as birth.

A second general point is that this creative diversification peculiar to conduct is especially evident in the multiplicity — or what might almost be called the pointless abundance — of solutions devised by closely related species when faced with the same problem. This is frequently seen even where a degree of conformity would in no way be harmful to the species concerned. It will be apparent, for example, if we think of all the known variations in the way birds build their nests, when the only really vital requirements are that there be sufficient concealment from predators and a minimal solidity for the sheltering of the young. Or again, we might think of the many and various types of spiders' webs, or of the variety of constructions to which social insects devote their energies. One can see, in such cases as these, the effects of a kind of behavioral flexibility (which encourages the exploration of successively opening avenues) much more easily than the result of selective processes imposing coercive conditions of survival. What then if each of these devised solutions had perforce to have been preceded by a great variety of purely random behavior patterns, among which processes of selection would have effected their sorting or sifting? Such examples show us what a serious calculation of possibilities, to account for each finally adopted solution, would give. It was a maxim of Herodotus that "if we are prodigals with time, all possibilities will come to pass." But we might answer here that elementary behavioral mechanisms have their precise function in saving a little of this time by employing trials and directed gropings rather than waiting upon the improbable factors of chance.

Third, the improbability of favorable chance circumstances would again increase exponentially if such chances had to operate on a double time-scale. First would

2. With the provision, of course, that this phenotypic behavior is the result from the outset of a genetic impulse or stimulus. This granted, though, where can such an impulse come from? Not from the environment, because this has no effect upon the genome. So there remains, once again, only the sacred element of chance. Yet this fish is compelled by chance not to founder on the land because a pond has dried up, but actively to "choose to explore the land." This is surely asking a great deal of chance: it would be necessary to ascribe all the features of a teleonomic behavior pattern to contingent circumstance.

have to come the formation of organs capable of particular uses; then the development of instincts or behavior patterns to make use of such organs would have to follow. First then, for instance, random mutations endow the woodpecker with its long beak, or the aphids with their sucking mouth-parts. There must then follow new and favorable random mutations, until the woodpecker goes in search of grubs in the wood and bark of trees and until the aphids come to live only on green plants with sufficient sap. It should be clear by now, to cut this short, that these organs and their corresponding behavior patterns must in each case have developed at the same time. Nor should there by any doubt of this with regard to plant life, since the reactional variation characteristic of an organ's modification in plants is itself the equivalent of behavior. The convergent reactional variations shown by plants in high-altitude habitats provide examples of this. Roots may be elongated (the alpine trefoil has flowers the same size as subalpine species, but has a relatively huge and tuberous root); stolons may be very differently formed (as in *Sempervivum montanum* compared with *tectorum*); plants may form thick cushions by agglomeration of individuals (*Androsace helvetica,* etc.); or there may be an increase in chlorophyll content, as we have seen in the case of our diminutive *Sedum.*

Having said this, our second major problem must be to understand how this simultaneous development of specialized organs and behavioral patterns has been able to ensure this kind of adaptation to particular habitats. In the case of apparently indifferent variations, the evolutionary model based on chance and subsequent selection remains intelligible, to be sure. Color changes, for example, may have the effect of increasing an animal's exposure to predators or may, on the contrary, improve its protection by effecting a kind of camouflage. Yet if woodpeckers, on the other hand, had no long beaks, aphids no sucking mouth-parts, they would quite simply gain their food in other ways. In cases such as these, therefore, the advantageous innovation has essentially been that of finding an unexploited habitat. It is this third variable, if one denies the causal role of behavior, which proves problematic. It makes the reliance on pure chance look even more unlikely as a solution, since chance must now effect a convergent combination of three distinct probabilities: that of a random morphogenetic variation, that of a chance variation in behavior, and that of a change of habitat fortuitously oriented towards least exploited areas.

We can see, therefore, that to introduce a certain generality in the process of the phenocopy would be to introduce a considerable simplification into these prob- · lems. This is because (as we have seen in the case of *Limnaea*) a phenotypic behavior pattern ensures at one and the same time both adaptation to a new habi- tat and the beginnings of transformation of the organ. Endogenous and genetic reconstructions occur only subsequently, by means of gropings directed into areas of organic disequilibrium — and there is no need at all for direct action by the environment upon the genome.

There is, we believe, a relative generality in our proposed model. But we must also make quite clear, in this conclusion, that the model is to be completed by the purely endogenous mechanism we have referred to as convergent reconstruction and extension.[3] This corresponds to reflecting abstraction on the cognitive plane and it is expressed in terms of organic development by all kinds of homologies. It would prove impossible, in practice, to explain the majority of instincts by reference to phenocopies. To do so would amount to attributing to initial phenotypic behavior patterns an intelligence markedly superior to that of the species concerned on this level. However, the concept of instinct that we have developed elsewhere[4] is worth mentioning here. Instinct is conceived of as a coordination of innate and transindividual schemes of action. It is thus analogous to the coordination of sensory-motor schemes, but is developed on the genetic plane or on that of epigenetic syntheses as directed by hereditary programming. Thus generalized, it is evident that such instinctive coordinations will depend not upon phenocopies, but upon these convergent reconstructions and extensions, and therefore upon varieties of homology, in the broad sense, which relate at once both to transformations of organs and to the associated behavior patterns. This may well, on the other hand, open the way for new and ever more varied and profitable combinations as is the case with reflective abstraction on the cognitive plane (where such combinations actually remain unconscious at elementary levels). If such openings occur, there is nothing to prevent the simpler initial schemes of action (which will later be combined) from structuring themselves by means of phenocopies. We have mentioned, as an example of an easily effected coordination of this type, the instinctive behavior of terrestrial mollusks which lay their eggs in the ground. Here the initial schemes involved are simply the animal's instinctive self-preservation in burying itself to escape drought or cold (in the winter especially), and the extension of this need for preservation or self-protection to the egg-laying itself, as an extension of the animal's activity. It is clear, of course, that so natural an action as this sheltering in the earth could just as easily be the result of phenotypic initiatives (and therefore of nonhereditary variations) as of any process of endogenous reconstruction. In this case, then, as far as initial schemes are concerned, nothing precludes a process involving a phenocopy.

The phenocopy clearly has limits in this respect. If we stick to indicating these limits and to invoking the very general mechanism of convergent reconstruction and extension, then we should be careful to emphasize that in fact a profound

---

3. [reconstructions convergentes avec dépassements].

4. In *Biology and Knowledge*, pp. 313-341.

unity exists between these two processes. The phenocopy, as we have ventured to interpret it, is the endogenous reconstruction of a phenotypic variation: its tendency is to remedy the disequilibriums which that phenotypic variation has allowed to subsist. Convergent reconstruction and extension is equally a matter of endogenous reconstructions, but these are brought to bear upon previous genetic constructions, recombining them according to later needs and lacunae. There is the same submission to the regulation and "preferences" of internal environment and epigenetic syntheses. The general mechanism which covers both these processes is therefore that of reequilibration or of maximizing equilibration. And it is in this direction, quite certainly, that the search for answers to the problems of evolution should proceed. Whether we are concerned with biological or with cognitive phenocopies, with convergent reconstruction and extension or homologies in the widest sense, the fact is we always find the same two processes at work. First there is requilibration by means of endogenous reconstruction. Second, (or in the same way in the case of organic phenocopies) there follows extension[5] or development beyond this initial reequilibration. This extension is achieved by means of reorganization involving new combinations, but where the elements recombined are derived from the preceding system which is now, as it were, overtaken. Maximizing equilibration itself, therefore, is no more than the expression of these two very general mechanisms. And even on the subject of the regulation of mutations, we find R. J. Britten and E. H. Davidson declaring that their model "provides for the possibility that innovation in evolution might arise through the combination, in new systems, of parts already functional in preexisting systems."[6] This was written in 1969, and the near relationship with what we had referred to two years before, as convergent reconstruction and extension is quite apparent.

From the most complex to the most simple, the processes clearly show us how far the role of chance is reduced to modest (though not negligible) proportions. It is, after all, precisely a property of assimilation, as a fundamental function of life, that it counteracts the element of chance in such a way as to make good use of it. One of the two central theses of neo-Darwinism, of course, is that all innovation is to be attributed to the random operation of chance. It is by a rather curious fidelity to this doctrine that H. Atlan, the biophysicist, has just produced a large book[7] in which he puts forth two very relevant concerns. On the one hand he summarizes (and adds to) the weight of evidence and interpretation which militates against (rather than supports) this concept of the role of chance. Yet he is nonetheless concerned, on the other hand, to present a defence of this same concept, to the

---

5. [un dépassement].

6. As quoted by H. Atlan in *Science*, 165 (1969), pp. 349-57.

7. *L'organisation biologique et la théorie de l'information*, as quoted in chapter 8.

effect that it is in fact capable of overcoming all these major difficulties. The role of the fortuitous, as Atlan reconstructs it, is summed up in the one phrase "organizational chance,"[8] and the arguments he deploys in its support are both numerous and convergent. This organizational chance is evident, for instance, in the reaction of self-organizing systems to "noise,"[9] or in the model of genetic regulation developed by Britten and Davidson. Or again, our own use of the idea of cognitive assimilation is summoned in support, and so on.

We can only follow with close interest the reasoning of so well-informed a theorist — but with some reservation as regards this central implication in his terminology. His organizational chance would have, on the contrary, to be called chance organized or reorganized by the living creature or the thinking subject. Organizational chance, after all, in Atlan's own terms, gives rise only to "disorganizations which are made up for," which are, in other words, compensated (or even over-compensated).[10] And "noise," moreover, though it diminishes the information available to an observer, will actually add to this information when it is transmitted within the system concerned (cf. the conducts α to γ, referred to in chapter 8, section III). The problem, in short, is that neo-Darwinism reasons as though the apple which chanced to fall beside Newton was the source of the great man's theories of gravitation. Atlan, on the other hand, provides all we need in order to understand how the apple's fall, a mere disturbing accident to any observer, became "organizational" in the subsequent internal transmissions within Newton's brain. And yet this only happened because, thanks to his earlier work and his powers of assimilation, he knew how to make it happen. The whole of this study could well be summed up by that concluding remark, since, in each of the domains addressed, Newton struggled to attain the prior conditions which were not random and were even necessary for his apparently aleatory inventions.

---

8. [hasard organizationnel].

9. See Atlan's summary, chapter 8, section III above.

10. [désorganisations rattrapées... surcompensées].

Index